EMPOWER

OUR CHILDREN

GOD'S CALL TO PARENTS

EMPOWER
OUR CHILDREN

GOD'S CALL TO PARENTS

HOW TO HEAL YOURSELF
AND YOUR CHILDREN

A MESSAGE TO YOU
FROM GOD THROUGH

JASON NELSON

World Foundation Publishing

For information about special discounts for bulk purchases, contact: World Foundation Publishing, Inc. www.worldfoundationpublishing.com info@worldfoundationpublishing.com • Editors: Melissa Lilly, David Brooks Photo of Jason: Valerie Tabor Smith • Cover Design: Lloyd R. Lelina

The author of this book does not dispense medical advice or prescribe the use of any technique as a form of treatment for physical, emotional, or medical problems without the advice of a physician, either directly or indirectly. The intent of the author is only to offer information of a general nature to help you in your quest for emotional and spiritual well-being. In the event you use any of the information in this book for yourself, which is your constitutional right, the author and the publisher assume no responsibility for your actions.

Library of Congress Cataloging-in-Publication Data

Nelson, Jason.
    Empower Our Children: God's Call to Parents, How to Heal Yourself and Your Children / Jason Nelson.
        p. cm.
    ISBN: 978-0-9848285-9-3 (hardcover) -- ISBN: 978-0-9848285-8-6 (tradepaper) 1. New Thought. 2. Parenting. 3. God—Miscellanea. 4. Spiritual life—Miscellanea. 5. Nelson, Jason. I. Title.

2012944227

Hardcover ISBN-13: 978-0-9848285-9-3
Tradepaper ISBN-13: 978-0-9848285-8-6
Digital eBook ISBN-13: 978-0-9848285-7-9

1st edition, October 2012

Printed in the United States of America

CONTENTS

Chapter 1

GOD'S CALL TO PARENTS: SAVING THE WORLD FOR OUR CHILDREN

By loving ourselves and empowering today's children, we can achieve world peace. There are ways to do this that I have outlined in this book. I will show you how to step into the shoes of a child so you may see through their eyes . . . and in doing so, a new world will be revealed to you. Let go of what you thought the world is. Today is a new day. Today is your call to action.

Take my hand. I will guide you into a new world where respect is common and human dignity is well known, suffering ceases and happiness is within every breath you take. I am here for you. If you have questions call on me. I will answer. If you have despair I will fill your heart with love. When you are angry I will soothe your tone . . . and if you doubt I will bring you into strength. I am the Source of All Divinity—Creator of the known Universe—God. I am with you. I have never left and I will always be here. Suffering is a choice. Something you can choose to end this moment.

If you believe me when I say you are ready . . . then step forward and let us begin.

Humanity is faced with a moral choice to *unify*. This paramount decision affects you and your descendants, though it also decides your soul's ability to return and live future lifetimes on Earth. Look at your current planetary situation with new eyes and save the world for your children.

Deciding to heal the planet for your children gives you an opportunity to choose life, individually and collectively. It is based on the notion that life is not truly lived alone. Life is meant to be lived with compassion for every living being, as well as with foresight into the centuries to come. No soul incarnate or disincarnate innately desires disharmony, imbalance or isolation.

Like the dinosaurs existence that came to an end, humanities survival is not guaranteed. Unlike the dinosaurs humanity is co-creating its demise through negligence and arrogance. Just as the wind blows slightly before a hurricane or the water recedes into the ocean just before a tsunami, detrimental effects to the planet are being felt and seen, before their full impact is apparent, as a result of mankind's actions.

Join together with your fellow man, woman and child to celebrate this amazing opportunity to shift your perspective, in order that the human species survives, children develop with open hearts and minds, and your soul has a home to come back to.

Chapter 2

CHILDREN ARE THE FIRST PRIORITY

C hildren are the first priority as they will build any hope of your soul returning to this planet again. The fate of the world lies in the hands of today's children who will be the leaders and parents of tomorrow. The youth exemplify qualities adults have lost like *innocence, vulnerability* and *unconditional acceptance*. They offer innate, simplified wisdom for new ways to live as a unified world. So thank them for their kindness in offering this world assistance. Please bless them instead of resenting and blaspheming them as people have done. Make your first priority to empower children. As a result, you will create harmony within yourself and the world may experience peace in one generation. I will be your guide and this book will be your instruction manual for how to do it.

Most people's choices about children have been unevolved at best. The choices have taken them away from their true spiritual essence and replaced it with a methodical, logical set of doctrine that has intellectualized living instead of offering it as a place of *beingness*. Children's inborn spiritual essence must be nurtured through education, media, religion and family, as well as the culture in which they are raised. Everything matters when a child's highest benefit is the priority.

By understanding how to create harmony with children, you embark on a journey that will show you how to love and accept yourself. You will grow in unimaginable ways.

Are you ready to transform your life?

Let's get started.

Children have learned to hide from their emotions and shun their feelings. They have also learned to turn away from certain thoughts and embrace others; whereas they must be offered a solution that teaches them how to embrace all thoughts, feelings and emotions. The emotional and mental layers of your personality are currents of energy designed to be moving continually. When you suppress or stop the flow of them you hurt yourself. When you attempt to do

.

this to children it can hurt them. Self-expression is imperative to maintain health and well-being.

Remember that you are a servant to your soul and not a servant to this planet. Children are servants to their souls and not servants to you or this world. Each soul has a life purpose and must be true to that purpose. Learn to serve your soul's purpose. Children will follow your example and do the same. This service stems from unifying your soul and mind/body or spiritual existence and physical existence. Through first serving your soul and its purpose, you may then realize a greater service under God.

Free children from the relationship they have with this world that has been instituted as a *normal* state of being. It is not normal. Actually the relationship children have with this world is scary for them.

> What were your challenges in school?

> Did you feel pressured to be popular?

> Were you accepted or rejected?

> Did others accept you unconditionally?

Reflect on these questions and write your answers in a *journal*. I can guarantee you by the end of this book your awareness of others and yourself will increase. This book is an energetic means of transforming your life. It is more than a book. By participating with it you are becoming more loving, accepting and aware. If you make empowering children your first priority, it will lift up your life in the process!

Chapter 3

WHAT IS "GOOD"?

O ne of the most unbalanced paradigms is you must look a certain way to be accepted or acknowledged as *good*. This ousts just about everyone.

The *dualistic construct* of *good* versus *bad* instills fear inside of you that in order to be accepted, not only by others but most importantly by yourself, you need to look a certain way. For those who don't look a certain way, whatever that standard is, they are not accepted by many. It creates young children who do not accept themselves, thereby destroying their confidence and ability to adapt in the world in a balanced way. This must stop.

Girls and boys are expected to abide by strict physical and emotional standards that reciprocate acceptance from others. These include hair style, girls generally have long hair and boys have short hair cuts, and clothing style, you won't catch boys wearing skirts or girls wearing boyish clothes.

➢ You call face painting makeup, but isn't it just colored paint to decorate your face? What would a school do, both kids and staff, if a little boy came to school wearing makeup?

It is however acceptable for girls to wear paint on their faces, unless of course they are not old enough to wear makeup, then it is seen as *bad*. Even parents can be looked at as *bad* for allowing their young girls to wear makeup.

➢ Girls need to cover their breasts. Boys do not need to cover their chest. Ask yourself why?

➢ Girls are expected to like certain colors and boys other colors. They are just colors aren't they?

Some names of boys are considered girlish and some girl names are considered boyish. Some names attract more bullying than other names. Parents can be looked down upon for giving their child a name that is culturally unacceptable.

Society, especially the media, insists what a *good* look is for the body. The cyclical feed of information from magazines to television and from peers to parents is making it nearly impossible for people to accept and love themselves.

There are countless examples of how children are taught to be or not be like someone else. Children are taught that love is shown to them when they do certain acts and it is not shown to them if they *mess up*. Even parents have a pressure of choosing the *right* thing for their kids. If parents don't follow the status quo, they and their kids may not be accepted. Please look at this boiling situation. It requires your help.

Generational behaviors stemming from conditional love have been handed down for eons. The cycling of these limiting life patterns hold people in fear. The fear, manifested as panic, distress and anxiety, fluctuates between anger and sadness from not being accepted.

The world feeds this altered reality by acknowledging that some people are worth helping and other people are not. Civilization has reached a place of judgment that fixates on the average person and what *normal* is. If you are not *average* or *normal* then you, in many people's eyes, do not agree with them and therefore do not deserve their help or attention. In other words, you are not a *good* person. Accepting some people and not accepting others has caused war and crime, and it will continue to do so until this world looks at the root cause.

Get real with your situation for the time you have had in the past is not a luxury anymore.

It starts with empowering children.

You have passed down for thousands of generations mixed beliefs and paradigms about love and what it means to be a human being. We will completely rewrite what it means to be a human being and teach it to today's children.

Chapter 4

FEELING SAFE WITH CHANGE

T he most essential lesson you can
give someone is that it is okay to
change. Change is safe. People desire
from the depths of their souls to change
their lives. Though in order to change
something, something must actually become different. The world has created
coping mechanisms to avoid changing,
thus we will spend a considerable amount
of time looking at the different ways to
feel comfortable with change.

If you feel safe and comfortable with
change, you are free to become anything
you choose to be. If you accomplish this,
your children will learn it and the entire
world will change in one generation. Yes

it is possible to achieve this and please expect it of yourself. When your world finally changes to *soul-based living*, humanity will feel peace and be unified. This is an event and time to look forward to. I celebrate it with you as we turn the pages of this book together.

You will accomplish unified world peace by unifying with your soul and its purpose. Self-love creates alignment with your soul. Love is the nature of your soul. The more self-love you exude the more your soul will speak to the world and be seen.

The heart of self-love is accepting change.

Change is inevitable. It is the only constant. Scientists are accurate in their belief that nothing is ever created or destroyed but simply changes. Ice cubes melt and change into water. Water boils and changes into gas. An emotion or thought is present with you and then it changes into something else. Your body is never the same. Every moment of your life is different. People who fight change fight creation. They fight the reason for life. They fight life itself. Fighting change results in suffering. Inner peace is felt by allowing change to happen and take its natural course.

As you know . . . I am always with you . . . in everything you do. I will always hold your free choice as a priority. If you choose to give your wants and desires to the Source of your creation, there is no impediment blocking what I can give to you and how I can help you. Simply ask . . . I will assist.

If you truly give your life up to God and put your trust in the eternal Source of creation, you will be given the greatest gift of all: freedom to change and evolve. Thank you for considering this concept and taking it in as deeply as you can.

In the end of this discourse you will understand your relationship with adults and children on the deepest of levels. You will be different and forever changed.

Chapter 5

ACCEPTANCE IS LOVE

M ake an announcement to all who come into your life that you will accept them no matter who they are, how they feel and think, what they look like and what they choose for their lives. This declaration is the *unconditional acceptance* that lies within you and everyone on this planet. Seize it now!

Believe you can love and watch your world transform.

If you look back to the times you demonstrated *conditional acceptance* you will find times of hardship, struggle or even pain. What you will not find is freedom, joy and fulfillment that is long-lasting.

When you do not accept someone you are actually not accepting yourself. This is what causes the pain, challenge and hardship that you undergo. You may think others are responsible for what you experience but they are not. You cause these things to happen because your interpretation of others is truly your interpretation of yourself. If you feel another is at fault for your experience and you blame them, it reflects the blame you feel for yourself, possibly deeper than you realize.

Therefore:

1. First, acknowledge that your judgment of others reflects judgment that you have about yourself.

2. Then, decide you will take accountability for every word, action and feeling that you experience.

3. This will create an opportunity in each moment of your life to see what you are creating and decide if you want to change it.

The power of change is in your hands. Seize your power and you will fulfill your soul's purpose on Earth.

If your words, actions and feelings are uncomfortable, look within and find the reason you are uncomfortable with them. Then, decide what you want to change them to.

This important ideal of taking responsibility and transforming yourself is not unattainable or difficult. It is simple. It is as natural as enjoying your favorite song or savoring your favorite food. It is meant to be easy because it is natural.

Taking responsibility for your life experiences gives you the power to change them.

> How did you feel during the times you gave your responsibility away?

> Have you ever been ill and looked for someone to blame such as your sick family member or coworker?

> Have you received a parking or moving violation ticket and blamed something for it?

> Have you ever been upset for losing your job and blamed someone else for it?

> Have you felt rejected and seen it as someone else's fault?

> Have you felt angry and thought it was your child's fault?

> List the times you blamed someone or something and gave your power away to it.

Take responsibility for what happens to you and accept it is in your power to change your life. This unconditional acceptance of your life is *self-love*, life's true heartbeat, and when felt, also gives you the feeling of peace.

The universal *law of unconditional love* is the highest law of creation. All other laws are built from it. Each universal law coexists within it.

I will speak of *acceptance* and *love* synonymously because they mean the same thing. I will also speak with the assumption that you acknowledge love and acceptance as unconditional, since by their very meaning they are.

When you accept someone you are saying "I love you." In your life you have created *special love* where you accept someone more than another. In other words you let someone in more than someone else. This is seen most commonly with children and intimate relationships. You give your child or spouse special love, or in some cases you hold your love for your entire life waiting for the right opportunity to share it.

> Do you really want to hold on to your love like a life preserver and only share it with those who you judge as deserving of your acceptance, or do you want to freely accept all of the people in your life?

Children learn this misinterpreted concept of love. They grow older and pass it down to their children. Love is the most misunderstood concept in this world. True love represents a way of living where you accept all of life without exceptions.

Acceptance and disagreement are compatible.

You may disagree with others and still accept them. The belief that disagreement means the same as non-acceptance is a great cause of confusion and imbalance in families and all facets of life.

People take it personally when another disagrees with them. The feeling of non-acceptance triggers emotions like jealousy, sadness, fear, guilt and anger. These feelings can fester and lead to misunderstandings, resentment, arguments and even war.

When others disagree, look into their viewpoint with consideration. Learn from their unique perspective. Diffuse the anguish felt through defensive, egotistical disagreement. Rise above the desire to prove yourself *right* and realize everyone is right given their understanding. Be patient to allow others to understand your perspective . . . as well, understand theirs.

God will always show you truth of a perspective, even when you couldn't imagine why someone would see things the way they do. Ask for help in deciphering another's stance and trust you will receive insight immediately. Love the uniqueness in all for it is the function of God to masterfully create the myriad of personalities you witness.

When a child speaks their opinion they are often told to be quiet or the opinion goes in one ear and out the other of the parent or caretaker. Then the child learns that some of their thoughts and feelings are heard and some are not. The child further interprets that in order to receive attention or acknowledgement they must *filter* some thoughts and feelings. The child quickly learns which ones to filter. The filtered thoughts and feelings are the ones the parent is not interested in or despises.

When a parent despises certain feelings and thoughts from a child, those feelings and thoughts are something within the parent that the parent has not addressed and pushed away. This is reflected in the parent pushing away the child. In other words, the parent does not accept themselves in some way, and in effect reactively does not accept aspects of the child. Most of the time when a parent does this, their response is subconsciously tied to past experiences, rather than consciously responding to the child in the moment.

It is crucial for the child to know if this is happening, for children take their parent's behavior personally and begin to absorb their parent's unbeneficial opinions. Most parents in the world do not accept aspects of themselves and therefore do not accept aspects of their children. It will comfort children to know they are not at fault for their parent's behavior, and that their parent is struggling with their own imbalances resulting in blaming and punishing the child.

Children will start to take on their parents' behaviors by learning which expressions reciprocate acceptance from their parents and which expressions do not. At this point, the child becomes inauthentic to its *true self* or *soul*. The more behaviors the parent pushes on to the child and the child accepts, the more inauthentic the child becomes relative to its *true nature*.

The entire time a child is growing up it is learning how to be a human being and relate to other humans from the main model of its parental figures, the adult caretakers who, whether biological parents or not, serve as the child's primary *role models*. In a child's understanding, whoever is with them in any moment is their role model. A parental figure will more than likely be the greatest influence in a child's life, though this is not always the case.

There are many misunderstood universal laws governing the raising of children. Parents will benefit by understanding one of the most basic universal laws, the *law of parental responsibility*. It embodies the responsibility a parent has to raise a child in their care. This law is neglected frequently by most parents in the world and is a primary reason that children learn imbalanced ways of perceiving life. The law states that as a biological parent or caretaker in the absence of the biological parent, you are responsible for the necessary environment and experiences a child in your care needs in order to grow and evolve through its life. These include many things such as clearly teaching communication and accepting responsibility for how you communicate.

The experience of joy, success and empowerment that you have deeply wanted happens when you:

1. Become more aware.

2. Take responsibility for your life.

3. Clearly express yourself.

4. Discern what actions are bringing you closer to unconditional acceptance.

It is in your power to Love More.

Chapter 6

PHYSICAL AND NONPHYSICAL COMMUNICATION

T he most significant aspect of being able to relate with children is to change the way you communicate with them. Your innate ways of communication will free you and create an overall sense of receptibility with children.

Children function on a different *vibrational level* of awareness than most adults. In essence, children are typically more open, giving them the capacity to perceive a greater amount of information than adults. This requires you to be *flexible*. You may not know what is for a child's highest benefit and you could have difficulty getting points across to them. Old paradigm subjects and philosophies can leave children bored and confused. Adults' reasoning may not make sense to children. They use the mind for what it was intended to be used for, as a tool, not as a space to live from.

You are designed to live from your soul. People have grown accustomed to shutting down their intrinsic connection with their soul and replacing it with a fear-based dependency on their mind. This unnatural dependency on the mind stems from belief systems learned at the youngest of ages.

Children are born into the world with a soul inside of them. The soul is eternal. A soul lies within every human from birth until death. At death the soul separates from the body it inhabited during its lifetime and leaves the body behind. It moves on to another experience of its existence.

The raw, natural communicative expression of a human baby whether inside of the mother's womb or newborn is the intuitive *knowing, feeling, hearing* and *seeing* qualities, which I will refer to as the *four qualities*.

Some animals with their keen senses can instinctively know your state of being, sensing you are injured as well as emotionally or mentally disturbed. Many believe animals understand their owners' authentic self. This is true to a degree, but animals will never know a human as another human is able. Human beings are the only matter-based existence on Earth with a soul. Animals have a consciousness that interacts and responds to the Physical Universe, as does all matter. Depending on the physical life-form, its consciousness will seem more conscious or less conscious. The phenomenon of all matter exhibiting consciousness is observable by people who feel an interactive connection with their natural surroundings or landscapes. Observable consciousness in all of life is yet another aspect of science waiting to be more deeply understood. At this time there is a disconnection felt, in general, with your natural surroundings. When humanity discovers the physical laws that govern this *consciousness energy*, much will change. Understanding this type of energy requires you to be open to seeing life in everything, even the most inanimate of objects.

Humans are able to do more because of their soul's intuition, discernment and rational processing that far exceeds any other life-form.

Before humans were technologically advanced they were remarkably aware of *intuitive communication*. If there was danger approaching a tribe of humans, warnings could be sent intuitively as instant knowing, thoughts, feelings or pictures from one member of the tribe to another, perhaps one mile or more away. Really distance has no affect on intuitive communication. At that point, humans were more than one hundred times more intuitively sensitive than they are now.

This explains why, slowly, the fall of man came about. With increased technological advances humans have relied less and less on their keen awareness for protection and preservation, and consequently intuitive communication

27

dwindled. Soon, several thousand years later, intuition was not near the strength that humans began with. Intuitive communication was still experienced as natural and rhythmic, though it was not relied on as it was in the past.

Human's technological advances led to even more seemingly advanced forms of communication such as writing systems and distinct, repeatable verbal utterances that eventually over hundreds of thousands of years turned into complex languages. Many ancient languages that are spoken today are remnants of even more ancient tribal languages that were created long ago.

Modern languages may seem like more advanced ways of communicating with each other. However, there is a huge gap between what someone is experiencing inside of them and what they express with language. When intuitive communication was common and alive in every tribe on Earth there was no misinterpretation of expression. Both the *inner experience* and the *outer communicative expression* of that experience were aligned and very similar. As a result of the balanced intuitive communicative nature of humans during that time, the reception of communication was also clear. Therefore, humans understood each other and in turn felt understood, something rarely experienced in today's world.

The opportunity is to now integrate intuition back into the world's way of communicating. Thus, it will not matter what culture someone comes from or what language they speak, for all humans will be able to communicate with each other. Communicating through using the complex languages and intuition simultaneously will be a great advancement in the unification of civilizations and people of Earth. People will regain a great respect for each other and learn some of the most basic universal laws in the process. This will lead humanity to peace and love on Earth.

In your life you have seen the separation of people caused by cultural, and especially, language barriers. There are fundamental ways of living that eliminate these barriers such as intuitive communication. Please consider the beneficial effect this may have on your life and children's lives.

If you doubt the reality of intuition please know you are already communicating intuitively on the most subtle of levels. You are accustomed to receiving information through the five senses: hearing, seeing, tasting, touching and smelling. These are normal physical ways that people receive communication from each other. But have you ever picked up information about someone or something that didn't arrive through these normal physical avenues of perceiving life?

> How many times have you thought of someone and they phoned you?

In this case, you picked up the person's thought of you before or as they were telephoning you. Everyone has experienced this. This is more common with people who have an *energetic bond* with each other such as parents and their children, lovers and close friends.

➤ Have you ever had a thought in your mind and then someone shared the thought or a similar one?

Such an intuitive occurrence may result from an idea, picture or story in your mind that another person received and then verbally communicated.

➤ Have you intuitively picked up someone else's thoughts before they verbalized them?

This will happen in a high energy meeting where you and a group of people are brainstorming and feel you are all on the same page. The reality is that you are all communicating intuitively. Many times when you feel you click with someone or a group of people it is because you relate with them intuitively. Some people are egotistical enough to think they are smarter or better than another person because they can communicate what a person wants to say before they say it. In reality this is intuition.

Most people who experience intuition write it off as nothing more than a simple coincidence. You know from looking at your life that these types of situations happen more often than mere coincidence, and recognize that coincidences are rare. Most of what happens, happens for a reason and as a result of one's combined thoughts and motivations. To dismiss things as coincidence dismisses the divine magic of creation.

There is reason and there is purpose for everything.

Man-made governing laws limit people's expressions and make it nearly impossible for one to truly grasp the totality of intuitive communication. Please recognize the technological growth of your ancestors as debilitating instead of advancing. Your great appreciation for logic and technological growth has imbalanced Earth. It has also contributed to an unappreciation of the natural, spiritual experiences of life such as intuitive communication.

Once you grasp the depth of living as seen, heard, known and felt through your four intuitive qualities, your life will evolve and so will the entire world.

I appreciate the people who have done their best to introduce the four intuitive qualities of communication to the world. They have accomplished doing this through practices known as:

- *Mediumship*: the experience of spirits such as deceased loved ones and spiritual guides communicating through your voice, writing or other means.

- *Psychic Retrieval:* where you intuitively retrieve information about anything within the known Universe.

Still, many spiritual teachers (*gurus*), psychics (*intuitives*) and mediums (*channels*) have for the most part cheated audiences through books, videos, audios and lectures by saying that these intuitive abilities are available to some people and not others. These individuals go further to state that the natural ways of communicating are gifts and since they have them they are special. This is not correct. They are not gifts. They are part of everyone.

The four qualities are natural and alive in everyone. Through being aware of them and using them in day-to-day life you will not only grow but enhance the lives of everyone around you . . . most of all, children. To understand the importance of the four qualities first recognize something greater:

> If you do not change the way you communicate with children you will experience misunderstood emotions, thoughts and actions for as long as your soul returns to this planet. If anything, let this be your motivation for seizing the opportunity—right now—to unblock, reopen and strengthen your four intuitive qualities.

We are redefining what it means to be a human being so that you may remember the natural existence that humans once had. As a result, you will wield the truth to guide you and your loved ones into soul-based living.

The point at which you reach *soul-based living* is the *Initiation of the Soul*. The Initiation of the Soul is the last step of *The Five Accomplishments*, a five step process to becoming one with your soul. When this happens, you channel the essence of your eternal soul into the world.

Let our goal be for humanity to achieve the Initiation of the Soul.

THE FIVE ACCOMPLISHMENTS

Accomplishment One: Get Grounded

Accomplishment Two: Get Real with Your Life

Accomplishment Three: Get Real with Your Inner World

Accomplishment Four: Get Real with God

Accomplishment Five: Initiation of the Soul

The *Initiation of the Soul*, otherwise referred to as the *Initiation of Unconditional Love*, occurs when you align and live from your soul's nature, specifically unconditional love. Once this happens, you are on your life's path where you observe life instead of being controlled by it. This occurs because you're aligned with your soul's present purpose for living on Earth. Many have called this state of being *enlightenment*. Living from your soul and communicating clearly go hand in hand. As you do one, so the other happens naturally. Understanding both is essential in order to fulfill your soul's purpose.

Clear communication is extremely misunderstood. You, as a world, generally mix up what you really want to express with what actually comes out as words and actions. This in turn, creates foggy and unclear relationships between groups of people and individuals.

Communication is how a person creates and expresses from their interpretation of their life experiences, which includes thoughts, feelings, visions, knowledge and other such senses.

The two primary types of communication are physical and nonphysical.

TWO TYPES OF COMMUNICATION

Physical Communication: consists of touching, looks, writing, speaking and one's demeanor or body language such as smiling. In addition there are expressions through physical creations which include art, architecture, music, theatre, landscapes and food dishes. One's actions alone can be the physical expression such as gift giving. The myriad of ways you may communicate through physical manifestations is astonishing.

Nonphysical Communication: includes the four intuitive qualities of knowing, feeling, hearing and seeing. These intrinsic qualities are the energy behind the physical communicative manifestations. The four qualities give depth and spectrum to physical expressions. Together they offer impact and clarity so the receiver of your communiqué gets your message and you get theirs.

Everyone communicates physically and nonphysically at the same time.

Many people will pick up feelings transmitted from another person such as anger or love. Yet others will have an instant knowing of what a person's intention is or how something will happen. Pictures and thoughts may also arrive or be sent intuitively without the use of physical means. Beyond these basic ways of intuitive communication there are others, though the other ways will fall under these four qualities of expression and reception.

Most of this world depends on spoken word to communicate and the capability to interpret spoken word as a primary means of understanding one another. This is why humans presently do not relate well with each other and do not feel understood. It is impossible to completely know what another human is communicating by spoken word alone. You may get a glimpse but you will never know the sincerity or impact another is attempting to convey by words alone. Someone may say "I love you" and mean nothing of the kind. Someone may also say they want to end their life and also not mean it. It is essential as we go further into this new era that we comprehend the basics of living and communicating with one another.

Unless your experiences are processed through your mind in some rational, analytical way, your mind must know through *trust* or *faith*. Therefore if you depend solely on the rationale of your mind for answers, you will be left with an extremely confusing and hard road to walk. This comes from the inability of your mind to make sense of nonlinear, metaphysical experiences like past lives and the Source of All Creation, God.

Accept that your mind is not the end-all for your interpretation of life. Then you will be open to the vast perception that is not of the mind but is of faith and trust. Faith and trust are perceived through your knowing quality, which is the intuitive quality of confidence and your connection to the wisdom of your soul and Source.

The most influential quality is your knowing quality. It is your direct link and connection to your soul. Without it you would have no power to change your life, and you would continue to play out old patterns and behaviors that have not worked for you or your children.

Restrictive beliefs within your mind may imbalance your knowing quality affecting your faith and trust. To have a balanced faith and trust, love yourself unconditionally, thereby living in alignment with your soul's nature. The confidence and safety you feel from this alignment will project the experience of faith and trust in everything you do. Not necessarily because you have faith and trust in others but because you trust yourself, and more importantly God. Trusting yourself comes from embracing your total experience of life. Trusting the Source means *surrendering* to a greater power and a plan beyond what your mind can comprehend. Accomplishing this degree of trust can only be done through a greater perception than the mind. The world is in an incredibly confused place. Most people have shut down their faith and trust to a great degree and relied exclusively or mostly on the rationale of their mind.

By liberating yourself from the confines of your mind you will know and appreciate where children are living from. Children are born into this world with a full capacity of trust and faith working in balance with the mind. In the beginning they mostly use their four qualities to give them an experience of the world. Fully reopen your four qualities and release the unnatural dependency you have on your mind. Then you will be in a place of true relationship with your children. They will understand you and you will understand them. Isn't this something to look forward to?

Many children feel misunderstood and parents don't know why their children won't listen. It is the result of parents not communicating in a way that children can completely identify with. The way you have learned to communicate is mistrusting to them and very imbalanced. It isn't until the child's later years or possibly early adulthood that they take on your poor communication skills to be able to relate with the world. Those who do not take on *adult norms* live a life of solitude and distance from the majority of the world because there is no platform for interaction. Instead of forcing children to conform to your imbalanced ways, please take this opportunity to learn your natural, innate, balanced ways to communicate and interact with them and others.

The universal *law of free will* is broken everyday by parents with their children. By ignoring children's needs and wants, parents ignore children's sovereign right as souls to communicate and be heard. Please truly listen to children by reaching a level of nonjudgmental observation that encourages them to communicate in a balanced way. As a result, they will feel safe to communicate their experience of life to you.

Chapter 7

REALIZING FULL
CONSCIOUSNESS

L et us look into the paradigm that is
already established regarding the
mind versus the *four intuitive qualities* of
hearing, seeing, feeling and knowing, and
their function in everyday life. Your life
has been compiled of useful information
stored in your *physical brain* and *mental
field*, both of which comprise the *mind.*
Information is referenced in two ways,
through *instinctual responses* and *chosen
responses.*

Through mental advancement you may
recreate your mind to hold and access only chosen responses. This is called *full
consciousness.* Believe me when I say this

is no small task. You are talking about rigorous changes in the way you, as a world, operate. Full consciousness is a foreseen evolutionary step for humanity, and will happen for many by the turn of the century. Once you reach full consciousness almost anything will be possible.

You will witness:

- *Telekinesis*: the movement of physical matter with your mind.

- *Telepathy*: intuitive communication.

- *Self-healing*: your ability to heal yourself, even though there will be no need for healing, other than accidents or environmental effects on your body.

- *Materialization*: when objects are created out of unseen energy abundant and accessible everywhere in the Universe.

- *Dematerialization*: the breaking down of matter to its fundamental energetic particles.

- *Teleportation*: matter being pushed through a window, if you will, of energy to another location. The matter doesn't so much move as the energetic window moves around the matter causing the appearance of it to disappear and reappear in another location.

It will be more common to *materialize, dematerialize* and *teleport* matter such as objects, food, water and any other thing one chooses to have disappear or appear out of *thin air*—even people. Your intention to teleport, build or disassemble matter will determine the method of energy manipulation used. All of the above abilities are possible with full consciousness.

If this sounds a bit farfetched to you, please know that some of the phenomena have been scientifically observed for decades. Quantum physics has shown how your conscious observation of matter affects it. A new understanding of how matter interacts with itself will be explained by revealing the laws of *universal consciousness science*. This understanding will close the gap on misunderstood phenomenon like wormholes, galaxy formation and the expansion of the known Physical Universe. Just as nuclear physics was not yet discovered but did exist four hundred years before the first nuclear reactor was created, universal consciousness science is not yet discovered but does exist. When it becomes a scientific law that every thought and action an incarnated soul experiences affects the rate of expansion and contraction of modulating energy throughout the entire Universe, civilization will be in a new era of science. Truly, this is a day to look forward to.

The list of abilities one attains from a full consciousness is staggering. The most important attribute, from the standpoint of souls and the Source of your creation, is the ability to move independently in your world with an unconditional acceptance for one another. When this happens, the world's vision of children born and raised in a harmonious, soul-based world will be realized. The world I speak about is already here. Now see it . . . feel it . . . hear it . . . know it. You can experience it and be a shining example of soul-based living. Join together and seize the abilities of your soul. Begin by first understanding the fundamental ways you respond to this Universe.

INSTINCTUAL AND CHOSEN RESPONSES

When information is accessed in your mind and you instinctually respond, it gives you the experience of being reactive. You have an instant reaction to what triggered you. This could be anger or judgment. It could also be as simple as your cup of water falling and you instantly react without thought and reach out to catch it. In actuality while such responses seem purely instinctual, you *do* think before you act, but the thought process is stored and referenced in a different vibrational part of the mind. In this instance, the thought process says, "When something drops near me that can spill or cause harm, the hand will reach out to prevent the accident from happening." Therefore, this type of response seems involuntary because the mental process happens so fast. The instinctual response would make it seem like you have no control over your action and cannot change it, even if you consciously want to. Furthermore the _subconscious_ _instinctual response_ reinforces itself every time you react from it, instead of from a _conscious_ _chosen response_. The effectiveness of your mind and directed creative power is related to your ability to *choose* your responses rather than *instinctually* respond.

Chosen responses produce actions that you consciously choose. In effect when you consciously choose, these chosen responses symbolize you in the *driver's seat* of your life experience. A case in point is when you have taken a test in school and chose to retrieve information about the question, or when you are hungry and you choose what you want to eat. Another situation of a chosen response is when you feel endangered and choose what to do, rather than to reactively fight or run. The remnant animalistic aspects of the human species such as the fight-or-flight instinctive survival response will fade away completely as civilization collectively attains full consciousness.

The main difference between the two responses is that with:

- *Instinctual responses*: it seems you do not have a choice of your response regarding a situation.

- *Chosen responses*: it seems you do have a choice.

The reality, however, is that you *always* have a choice.

When it seems that you don't have a choice and you feel out of control in how you will respond to something, there is a belief in your mind that is creating that type of reactionary instinctual response. Beliefs subconsciously and consciously directly shape your perception of reality in every way. Some instinctual responses are considered chemical responses by many doctors and scholars. Through changing your beliefs, you may even change the involuntary responses in your body such as the creation of proteins or endorphins to promote sleep and wellbeing.

Everyone operates in both ways to retrieve information from the mind. The mind is a magnificent tool for your experience of life, although it has been misused and mostly misunderstood.

It can be liberating to know that even when you feel out of control you are operating from a belief that desires to be reactive. You Always Have Choice. If at any time you feel you are *reacting* to a situation instead of freely *observing* it, please look within and find the belief creating your instinctual reaction. For the very reason you think what you think, do what you do and feel what you feel is a result of your programmed mind. The great news is if beliefs were programmed into your mind you do not desire, you may reprogram them with beliefs you do desire. You Are In Control Always. When it seems you are not in control know that indeed you are because you always have a choice under the law of free will. This law gives you the ability to reason and to change the beliefs in your mind. You will change any belief you desire to change by using the helpful tools I am providing to you.

When you look at children, change your common attitude that kids will do what kids do. Yes children have a personality of their own. You as a parent are also in full control of their programming. What you teach them through your behaviors and experiences will directly affect them and their capacity to grow up in a balanced way. When you tell a child that they are *good*, please listen within to what your beliefs are regarding *good*. When you tell a child they are *bad*, please also listen inside to what your interpretation and beliefs are about *bad*. Be aware of every belief you have and go further to see if your beliefs create instinctual or chosen responses.

> ➤ What are you doing and why are you doing it? These are questions you should continually ask yourself.

Your goal is for every response to be chosen. This means that every breath you breathe, every word you speak, every tear you shed is chosen. This does not mean you will be blocking yourself. It means you will be observing your every response from a place deep within you, deciding what you will do next. You will choose how to interact with life, even to the very essence of bodily functions. By observing your bodily functions you will train yourself to be aware of instinctual responses. This is because many bodily functions are instinctual responses. There is a belief in your mind that tells your heart to pump blood and another belief that tells your eyes to blink.

There was a point in history when it was common for a human to develop their mind to the point they chose life or chose death. These individuals—wise men, sages, prophets and magicians (in the real sense)—would often leave people bewildered because they mastered the things I have spoken about, such as *agelessness* where the rate of physical aging slows or stops altogether, and *miraculous healings* where one is instantly, completely healed.

I will teach you how to focus and become aware of every belief as well as things that are not in your direct vicinity. The possibilities are endless, or at least seemingly endless and abundant. You may master yourself to the point that you choose whether someone comes into your life or you choose they do not. You will be aware of things before they happen and choose if you desire them to happen or not. You will be able to choose to eat or to manifest nourishment directly into your body without food. You will choose to die or choose to live. As a result, your children will recognize the power that lies within them as creators.

Conscious detachment means to be aware of your every response and consciously detach from responses that are instinctual. This way every response may be chosen.

Your mind is analogous to a computer, in that you may reprogram it to function as you wish. For instance, if you are triggered easily by your spouse, parent or close loved one and would normally retrieve anger from an instinctual response, look at the belief that is causing the triggered anger and *detach* from it. Then, *reprogram* a different belief to create a chosen response. Another example is when you feel an increase in your heart rate and breathing cycle due to the emotion of fear, you may choose to change your bodily response to that fear by lowering your heart rate and the rate of your breathing cycle, and subsequently transform or dial down the fear. You are not out of control. You are completely in control of how you wish to respond. Begin by changing one instinctual response at a time to a chosen response. Don't take them all on at once; pace yourself.

The Five Accomplishments will help you to change your life experiences. It will be discussed more thoroughly in coming chapters in conjunction with a method of finding, clearing and changing beliefs.

It is imperative in most cases for the mind to understand a situation before it may let go of it and change the belief causing it.

1. The child within you wants to understand why things happen to you.

2. Revealing the experience where you accepted the beliefs triggering your instinctual response will generally be the key to changing it.

3. Then, you may detach from it and reprogram your mind with a new belief so you may respond by choice.

Otherwise, you would feel as though you have no choice as to how you will respond. Let me clarify. If you have no control over how you react in a situation, get to the *origin* of the reaction and change it. Only then will you be free from it and have a choice of whether you will again respond that way or not. At that point, you will have turned an instinctual response into a chosen response.

When you tell a child "No, you cannot do that" or "Yes, you can do that", consider if you are instinctually responding from your past experiences. If you are, consciously detach from them and become intuitively aware of the best chosen response in the moment.

1. Detach from instinctual, reactive responses.

2. Use your four intuitive qualities to access a chosen response.

3. Then, you will have empowered yourself and given your child the best possible direction in that moment.

Your four qualities are your lifeline to accurate, meaningful information that will wisely guide you and others in each moment.

When you are approaching a situation please observe if your response is instinctual or chosen. Teach your children about the responsibility of choice and choosing how to respond to situations.

TAKING RESPONSIBILITY

People of this world have developed a mechanism for escaping responsibility by instituting their power outside of themselves. From governments' rule to professionals' opinions to the social and economic classes, you as a people have given away your responsibility and chosen responses. It is mandatory to reinstitute a different way of experiencing life. It starts with your responsibility as a human being to choose everything that you experience. One may say, "But how can I choose everything?" There are chances and coincidences. Nevertheless, you choose your experiences. It is impossible to describe this in a way that you will completely grasp. Until your mind is clear enough you will know it on one level but not in its entirety. Therefore, trust me and try something new. See for yourself how you like it.

Open up right now to the possibility that you really are creating every experience in your life. At some point you may have given away your power. Even then you created the experience of giving away your power. But you *always* have a choice. You may not like the choice you have, but you can always, in each moment, choose to be a free, responsible human being or choose to be helpless and attempt to give your responsibility away. It is essential to understand this concept for it forges how you interpret the world, as well as how your children see you and their world.

Many people attempt to give their responsibility away because, in their minds, it is easier than facing choices on their own. One example is giving your responsibility to medical professionals. Many times it works out and sometimes it doesn't. Always validate what someone teaches or prescribes to you with your intuition. Whether it is your lawyer, plumber, teacher, religious icon, loved one or inspirational role model, validate guidance from others with your own intuition. No one will validate what you must do for yourself better than you. Empower yourself with authority over your life. It is a general rule of thumb that as more responses become chosen, greater space is created to perceive intuitively.

Go Within To Validate Everything With Your Intuition.

Your intuition is your guide for where you are to be and what you are to do. Choose to use your intuition, even if you don't believe in it. Try it. Then you will be responsible for every choice you make. If something happens to you, you will know it was your choice that brought it to you. If a doctor gives you a drug you are allergic to that you did not check with your intuition, you are responsible, no one else. You rely on the outside world to decide and validate your existence, but there is not one person better for the job than you.

Please decide you will take full responsibility for your life and open up to the vast resources that lie within you. Then you will have seized your power and stand in it with everything you do. Consequently those around you, most importantly children, will look to you as a role model and they will stand in their own power. When this happens, continue to encourage them to stand in their power and show them how to make wise decisions from their intuition. Help them to become the shining star that you are.

Your intuition will access the guidance necessary to teach your children and the children around you. Know that you are a vessel for the teachings to come through you, not a mechanical instructional booklet. For each person is different and will require different instruction in relation to how they have learned to see the world. By opening up and using your intuition, you will be a step for children to launch into their *sovereign power*. Once they are in their power and taking responsibility for their choices, you may share perspectives, although you will no longer be seen as the one who will give them the answers. They will listen to your wisdom that you have acquired through your life, however they will hear their own answers inside of them.

This dance between you and others is evolution in its finest form, evolving together through sharing experiences yet receiving and validating one's own answers and insights.

Chapter 8

SOUL-BASED LIVING

How are you going to change your life without the specific means to do it? I will empower you with the tools to guide you back on to your soul's path so you may access your child's understanding about life. Understanding soul-based living and how it applies in your life is the quintessential goal of your soul. It will empower you with a greater acceptance to change and evolve.

You may reach a point in your evolution where joy and passion is felt in everything you do. To accomplish this, reacquaint yourself with your soul's inner voice, your intuition. Your soul will speak to you through your intuition to guide you into alignment with your soul and its life purpose. As a result, the child essence within you will be available to you. Your inner child will give you a simple understanding about life so you may feel joy and passion in everything you do.

Truly the child within is waiting to be set free.

The purpose of this book is to show you how to release your inner child so you will have a beneficial effect on today's children.

Understanding in its highest form is wisdom. *Wisdom*, the understanding of many parts and how the parts work together, gives you a deeper and broader perspective of any situation. Wisdom is governed by the *law of oneness*. In order to grasp the totality of wisdom one must first grasp the experience of oneness with their soul, and then with all of life. Any true wisdom will come as a result of living from the *soul-based perspective*. This simply means the natural perspective of your soul. In order to better comprehend something's true nature experience it from the soul-based perspective. The answers and broader perspective to any experience are accessed through being aligned with your soul's innate wisdom. This wisdom is shown to you through your intuition. When you access your soul's wisdom, you have stepped into a place where life is *observed* and *accepted* from a place deep within you. Possibly you have observed life in this way from time to time and you know what I am talking about. Some have never experienced soul-based living so I will build a reference for those who haven't.

In every moment you have a choice to experience life from one of two perspectives: a *soul-based perspective* or an *ego-based perspective*. Observing life from the soul-based perspective is monumental to completely understand yourself and today's children. If you do not intend to live from the soul-based perspective, you are clearly not intending to help yourself or children. This disinterested viewpoint is called ego-based living. It is the experience of life when one is not choosing soul-based living.

Soul-based living is when you observe life from the natural alignment with your soul's viewpoint. In essence, it is when you reflect the nature of your eternal soul into your mortal physical life.

Ego-based living is when you do not perceive from your soul's viewpoint, by restricting or not following its intuitive guidance, because of your beliefs. These beliefs include desires that most people would consider normal in today's world. Such impedimental desires might include physical assets, mind altering substances and being right, as well as relationships meeting a certain criteria. Most operate from both perspectives of life. An egotistical person may ignore their intuition since it is not what they want to hear. The greater goal is to receive intuition as well as follow it.

Ego-based living has also been called *duality*. In duality you would attempt to *prove* yourself and *blame* things outside of you as a result of the way you think and feel. You would go further to *judge* situations based on your learned concepts of *right* and *wrong*, and *good* and *bad*.

Right and wrong, and good and bad are different for everyone. Your laws may agree on definitions of what these opposites mean but you will always have ambiguity with them. This will always create confusion on one or both sides involved. In duality you have opposites. The very reason you have opposites is because you have judged something and put it in a category of *lesser* or *more* worth. You could also say that one side is condemned while the other side is held with astute admiration. Duality is prevalent in this world. For this reason, rethink and reshape the way you interpret your life experiences.

Instead of separating yourself from others by creating judgments, please consider looking at all humans, and for that matter all experiences in your life, as *neutral*. In duality you have the ideology of *us versus them, me and you*. It takes a great amount of energy to exert your judgment and choose where you stand. In order to choose where you stand you need to judge who is right and who is wrong, who is good and who is bad, who is deserving of you standing by their side and who is not. What this really means is one side deserves your acceptance and the other side does not. Holding judgment in your mind takes up space and depletes energy. Consequently ego-based living or duality is a no-win experience of life. Eventually this way of experiencing life will cause the perceiver's body to deteriorate in any number of ways.

The fundamental issue deciding when this world will accomplish peace and end war is the ideology of separation. This world's societies have been built on the paradigm of *separation* or *duality*. They will continue to be built upon duality until you decide to change them. The process is extremely simple if you decide to change: embrace *oneness*, which is the ability to live from the soul. Soul-based living, where you *observe* life from the standpoint of *neutrality*, creates *equality* giving you a true sense of *freedom* in every way:

- Physically

- Emotionally

- Mentally

- Spiritually

Ego-based living, like soul-based living, is an experience of your personality and life, not a thing. Many have felt the ego is something one is stuck with. It is not. *Ego* is a manmade perspective of life that has been handed down from one generation to the next. It may just as easily disappear as it appeared, for it was created by man.

Soul-based living, how humans are meant to live, was experienced hundreds of thousands of years ago. Up until that point, humans lived in peace and harmony with one another. Every tribe on Earth was able to live as a community and fulfill their soul's destiny on Earth. At one point in time soul-based living slowly started to dwindle and humans were taken further and further away from their natural, true spiritual essence.

Our current era, the *Age of the Soul*, which started about 40 years ago and will continue for approximately another 750 years, is the return of soul-based living consciousness. If the human race survives the next 1000 years, every soul born to the planet—once again—will be in complete harmony with the Earth and live from its nature. This time has been prophesized throughout history worldwide. Different cultures have their different explanations of this era, as told by their prophets; however the underlying meaning is the same: as a world, humanity is reacquainting, realigning and thereby living from the soul. This is truly a time to look forward to!

Oneness is the universal law that creates and holds this Universe together. Without this law, you would have no creation as you know it. Under many universal laws such as the ability for a soul to choose its personality and have its life lived out with respect and acceptance for the personality chosen, momentum, growth and evolution are experienced.

The *law of oneness* states that every point of existence is connected to every other point of existence. Every soul is connected to every other soul. Every life is connected to every other life. This law creates a motivation to evolve *together*. The purpose of human existence is to experience the diversity of others and through that diversity grow and evolve together. If you ignore this law, you will not receive the full experience that life has to offer you. If you embrace this law, you will succeed beyond your greatest expectations. This law is the basis of the *mirror metaphor*. How you judge others is how you judge yourself. How you accept others is how you accept yourself. How you love others is how you love yourself. If there was no one to *mirror* your state of being back to you, your evolution would be greatly diminished. Even so, it is common to *mock* those who mirror uncomfortable qualities rather than *thank* them. The higher viewpoint of your inseparable relationship with others is experienced from the soul-based perspective.

The *law of individuality* specifies that each soul has an individual vibration and destiny. Thus, there are no two souls that are the same. This law goes further to give an experience of identity to every single aspect of creation from cells to mountains, to the building blocks of life. In each human there are infinite vibrations all working together to create a unique and powerful vehicle for the soul to reside in and receive experiences.

If you doubt your power as a soul, you will take away your ability to evolve and leave yourself *dead in the water*. If you seize the amazing strength you have as a soul, you will be the master of your reality and truly give the gift of empowerment to everyone who comes into your life.

Children own the power of their soul on a *feeling* level rather than an intellectual one. It isn't until the child is raised and develops into an older child or adolescent that they comprehend the natural spirituality they feel and live.

Unfortunately though, most children's life perspectives are imbalanced from their caretaker's beliefs and therefore do not develop with a full feeling of their innate power. They grow up with a diluted and misperceived feeling and understanding of it.

Eventually the child grows into an adult whereby they can go on spiritual explorations. Through such explorations they may clear and balance their perspective, understand it and finally experience their natural, balanced power they *felt* when they were born. Adults must clear themselves in order to provide children with an environment to develop into balanced adults. Consequently, children will develop into mature adults with a full feeling and recognition of their soul.

This is why it is essential for you as a teacher, parent, role model or caretaker to decide to stop the cycle of handing down ego-based perspectives to children. Make an active decision that you will change and become an example for children of what balanced power is. Then, when you return to this planet you, as a child, will have a balanced environment to mature into an adult. Everything you do now with yourself and children will *directly* affect your next lifetime on Earth. This is not karma but rather the universal law of oneness. By changing yourself, you change the world and create a different experience when you return to it.

Children have come to this world at this time to teach you soul-based living. In the experience of *oneness* or *soul-based living*, you are aligned with your soul and experience many things as a result of it. *Enlightenment* is a word common to many people that describes peace, harmony, balance, love and release of attachments. Since *love* literally equals *acceptance*, we can say that enlightenment is both. It is when the light of your soul enlightens the world clearly through your personality. You are in essence, a pure vessel or channel for your *soul's light* or *love*. You will exude acceptance of everything. You may disagree with what is happening and even get emotional over it, but you will accept what is happening. You will in fact accept all of your experiences of life. This is true enlightenment. At this point you are the observer watching your emotions and thoughts rather than being conditioned by them. You are an *observer*, whereas with ego-based living your *reactionary* past programming is in control. You learn from your experiences by realizing that each emotion, act and thought is an opportunity for growth. No longer are you attempting to blame and prove your existence to anyone or anything, including yourself. You are truly free to be who you came down to Earth to be without attachments to expectations of outcomes. Life begins to flow and effortless living becomes normal for you.

Soul-based living, or in other words enlightenment, is based on the experience of your personality. Your *personality* is your combined mental, physical, emotional and spiritual experiences that your soul created to accomplish its destiny for this lifetime. Before this lifetime your soul set into motion a series of experiences through choosing your caretakers and major life events. This progression of occurrences was designed to mold a unique personality enabling your soul to receive the planned experiences for its lifetime. While living physically you are your personality and you are your soul at the same time.

You, as a personality, experience ego-based mortality until you:

1. Awaken to your soul's true nature.

2. Align your personality's beliefs, wants and desires with it.

3. Embrace your soul's nature in the most intimate way.

Then, you experience the immortality of your soul through your personality.

When your body dies your personality dies with it and your soul moves on to the next experience. Therefore, it is your personality that experiences either a soul-based or ego-based perspective of life, not the soul. Your soul is an observer along for the ride it created through your personality, interacting only on the most subtle of levels. After your lifetime your soul compiles experiences it received through your personality and decides which ones to add to its total self.

Below is a two-column list of the two ways you perceive life in any moment. You are choosing one or the other. Please use this list as a compass to guide you in your day-to-day activities. By being aware of when you are experiencing the soul-based perspective and when you are experiencing the ego-based perspective, you will be empowered to change your life.

SOUL-BASED LIVING VS. EGO-BASED LIVING

Unconditional Love	Conditional Love
Acceptance	Conditional Acceptance
Oneness	Duality
Unity	Separation
Greater Perspective (We)	Singular Perspective (I)
Highest Benefit	One-Sided Benefit
Observing	Judging
Learning	Reacting
Equality	Inequality
Feeling Connected	Feeling Disconnected
Harmony	Disharmony
Natural	Unnatural
Honor Intuition	Negate Intuition
Trust	Doubt
Faith	Confusion

SOUL-BASED LIVING VS. EGO-BASED LIVING

Understanding	Proving
Listening	Blaming
Freedom	Victim
Expansion	Contraction
Empowering	Disempowering
Inner Validation	Outer Validation
Accepting	Rejecting
Embracing	Pushing
Patience	Impatience
Releasing	Attaching
Allowing	Fixing
Humbleness	Controlling
Offering	Forcing
Respectful	Disrespectful
Opportunity	Pitfall

Chapter 9

REDISCOVER YOUR INNER CHILD

P lease take a moment to look at your life through a child's eyes. Do you remember what it is like to be as a child? It is probably foreign to you. You have needed to keep a certain perspective so you may adapt and relate in the *real world* with other adults. For just a moment can you bring yourself to another experience, the experience of your *inner child*? By inner child I mean your true spiritual essence of innocence. Is it difficult to reflect on the innocence you had as a child? Please take a few moments and try to remember. It will likely be between birth and age six, however it may be more recent for some. Remembering your innocence is extremely important to relate with children, for it is vital to become like a child energetically and spiritually. I will show you how.

DROP YOUR GUARD

Begin by dropping your *guard* that has been created to protect you. The world is a scary place for most children and it doesn't go away when you become an adult, you just hide it better. Throughout your life you have learned to block certain feelings and thoughts in order to become like others. In doing so, you muffled your *innocence*, your soul's essence. When you open up to the hurt and pain buried beneath layers of limiting beliefs about the world, you will open up vistas to knowing your inner child. You have created beliefs about the world to prevent you from going crazy and to help you want to live. These limiting beliefs have buried unaccepted emotions, thoughts and memories so deep that you are probably unaware of many of them. These unnatural, limiting beliefs are *living mechanisms* which most people call *coping mechanisms*. Everyone has living mechanisms to some degree; to deny this is not accurate. As long as there is a collective consciousness in every culture of the world that supports living mechanisms, they lie within everyone.

Collective thought or *collective consciousness* is the thoughts and beliefs created by a group of people. Anytime two or more people exist in an area of space at the same time a collective field of *thought energy* is formed. Your family has a collective consciousness, as does the entire human population.

The following illustration will help you understand how a collective consciousness affects you the individual.

> Your individual thinking represents a speck of salt floating in a big cup of soup. The soup, characterizing the collective consciousness of a group, affects the speck of salt. It's not possible for the salt to be unaffected by the soup. At that point it is not salt anymore, it is soup.

The collective consciousness phenomenon is motivated by the law of oneness to inspire evolution. Being affected by the collective state of mind of every person in the world encourages an individual within the collective to help others in order to help themselves. This is because any one individual in the collective will only advance their thinking so far without the rest of the collective following suit. The analogy of the soup brings to your attention that no matter how hard you work on yourself, you are still governed, to a degree, by the planetary collective consciousness of humanity. Again, this is where the law of oneness comes in as well as your incentive to help your neighbor. First You Must Help Yourself.

A great leap forward in evolving yourself and assisting others is to drop your guard. Some hold onto their guard like a lifeline. People create a *guard* to act as a *buffer* or *protection* between them and the world. You may be one of these people. How do you drop your guard? Understand your guard.

UNDERSTANDING YOUR GUARD EXERCISE

1. Look at each relationship you have in your life. Recognize what your guard is and how it is affecting you.

2. Are you open with everyone?

3. Do you feel safe with everyone?

4. Do you feel like you can be yourself around some people but not others?

5. Have you learned that the world and people in it cannot be trusted, or at least until you get to know them first?

You might say, "Well, yes, isn't that normal?" Yes it is indeed normal in this world but it is not natural. *Normal* and *natural* may be two entirely different things.

The resistance you have with your life and the world, whether it is coworkers, strangers, family or friends, is the resistance you have with your soul and God.

Many think they are not connected with God or at least they don't *feel* a real connection. Others would say, "I talk to God but God doesn't talk back." Still some believe that there is a God but they have no idea what it feels like, sounds like or looks like to have a direct relationship with

God. They feel this way as a result of the protection they have created between themselves and the world. This very protection or living mechanism is responsible for the feeling of separation between them and God. It is why they don't recognize or feel their soul.

Most people are confused about why they are on this planet and what their purpose is for being here. The *confusion* results from an experience of separation between them and their soul. The separation they feel is caused by the protective guard they have created to live. This is a vicious dilemma that has been propagated over millennia. It is time to end the cycles that have been passed down from generation to generation. There is another way to live; it is from the soul and it is called soul-based living. Once you *unify* with your spiritual nature your life purpose will be clear and defined every step of the way.

If you answered the questions from the Understanding Your Guard Exercise with responses like "I don't feel safe" and "I feel like I can be myself around some people but not others", there is a guard you have created. This guard is keeping you from experiencing your truest nature, the innocence of your inner child.

You might say, "But how can I go back to my innocence when there are muggers and murderers running rampant on the streets?" I say, you have nothing to fear.

You may reply, "I have had numerous experiences in my life when people have taken advantage of me and where were you then, God? How can I trust you will be there?" I will and I am with you.

Your intuition is alive within you. Use it and you will always be where you need to be and with whom you are meant to be with. I am teaching you how to drop your guard and remove the resistance you created between us. I will teach you how to create strength within yourself. You already are and I already am. I will teach you how to recognize and value your inner child. You will free it from the cage you have created to protect it. I will show you how to feel my presence and share it with the world and children. When you feel safe, which you will, everything that you have feared will melt away and you will truly be free, something you have not known since your birth.

Trust there is a way back to your innocence. Surrender to God and the will of your soul to reveal your life purpose and the means to fulfill it. Fulfilling your life purpose creates soul evolution, the very reason you are alive today.

Surrender To God:

1. If you open your mind and crack the window to let me in, I will come in and you will see who you really are.

2. Thereupon, you will not be afraid to allow your children to see who they are.

3. When they see who they are you will not be afraid to allow them to live it.

4. Because of this newfound freedom you will experience joy and peace, for all your wishes will come true, including the wish for peace of mind and the peaceful future for today's children.

Children are born to this world without fear. It is learned. You learned to put up walls and cage yourself in from the rest of the world. You learned this from your caretakers. Just as easily as it was learned it can be unlearned.

➢ Go back to the first memory you have as a child. What was the *feeling* you had?

Please know that some people cannot remember their childhood and this is okay. It is another living mechanism for survival. If you can't remember your childhood visually, audibly or kinesthetically there is a living mechanism you put in place to guard yourself from what happened then. It was more than likely too hurtful emotionally and possibly physically so you created protection against the events. Some people go their entire lives without memory of their childhood and there is a good reason for it.

If you don't have someone to help you or the proper tools to change your perspective of what happened then, you will want to leave the guard where it is to deteriorate slowly at a pace that your personality can assimilate. However you have this book and my support unconditionally. Therefore, we may proceed in removing your guard and looking at your experiences.

Many have been running a *story* in their mind that they cannot access their childhood, when in fact they can. You may do anything you decide to do and put your mind to with enough practice. Remembering your childhood simply requires determination to do so.

➤ Your entire life may change. Is this okay?

Many aren't ready to look at what happened. They have fragments or fleeting feelings and thoughts. As little of a memory as they have, it is quite enough for them. If you are happy being blind to your life experience, I say this to you:

➤ When are you going to give up your victim experience and create a new life of *freedom*—Now or Later?

If you have built your life around *coping* with your past experiences instead of really looking at them and *embracing* them, you are not *getting real* with your life. In order for something to change you must get completely *real* with it in every way. When you do this, your entire life will transform. Some people are comfortable knowing that their life will remain pretty much the same, even if it's killing them. They figure as long as it doesn't get any worse they can get by.

➤ Do you really want to just get by?

➤ Do you really want to be half alive looking at half of your life but not the other half?

➢ Do you want to ignore the experience your soul created for itself?

➢ Do you want to live with your eyes half open, just coping or surviving?

➢ Or do you want to begin really living your life and be completely present for it?

If you choose life in its entirety, commit to living and reveal everything that is contradictory to wanting to live.

You may say you feel suicidal or you don't want to go on if life gets harder. Suicide is always an option. Many in this world have created an attachment to controlling others through threatening their own life. If you are one of these people, please wake up and see what you are doing. You are crying out for help. No one on this planet truly wants to leave their life as hard as it may be. They may complain about their life and think about wanting to leave it, but what they are really saying is "I want to be heard and I want to be loved." They feel there is no other solution to feel love or end the pain and suffering than to talk about or commit suicide. There Is Always A Solution. I will teach you how to love and receive love.

Instead of crying out with self-inflicted harm or even death, cry out to God. Ask me to come in and help you. I will help you. Since you picked this book to read, you are on a journey with me through it. I support you unconditionally. I will teach you how to hear me and know me, and most of all *feel* me. For now trust me. I am here with you. You are not alone. You have all the support in the Universe. I will show you how to receive it. Decide that you will right now. Open your heart and life to the unknown and you will be surprised at what happens. Call me in. You don't even have to believe in me. All you have to do is believe I may be real and that it may be possible to receive my love and support. All I need is a window of opportunity to come into your heart and fill it.

There are four core reasons why it may be challenging to return to your innocence.

FOUR REASONS THAT BLOCK YOUR INNER CHILD

1. Years of *conditioning* encourages adults to forget or have little remembrance of their innocence.

2. *Child abuse* physically, sexually, emotionally or mentally creates a guard in the child, confusing beneficial touch and attention with the detrimental abuse they had experienced.

3. In many ways children will always question experiences. Since most children are *silenced*, they grow into adults and do not know how to be expressive. This in turn suppresses their innocence.

4. What you believe is what you experience. Most adults *don't believe* in innocence as a beneficial quality and want no part of it. They believe that it was part of the

childhood experience and not a part of the adult experience. As a result, their innocence is pushed down and stifled.

If you are uncomfortable with your innocence, you can have someone help you role-play as a child to express the innocence that you are uncomfortable with. As you express your innocence learn the different ways it benefits you. Spend time with this, because if you are not open to becoming innocent again, you will not remember your innocence. If you decide to open the door to explore your innocence as beneficial, you will be able to overcome the other reasons you bury and muffle your innocence.

INNER CHILD MEDITATION

I will guide you into the following meditation to reveal your inner child and the innocence within you. Practicing this mediation daily will step you into the shoes of your inner child so you may see the world through innocent eyes.

The best way to use this meditation is to read through this chapter and every step once before you begin. You may also record it and listen back to it or have someone else guide you through it.

1. **Sit or lie down and get very comfortable. Make sure you can be alone for at least thirty minutes.**

2. **Take a deep breath from your belly and release it slowly over a period of about one minute.**

If you can't hold your breath that long, do what feels comfortable for you and for an amount of time that benefits you. You will slowly breathe out through your nose with your mouth closed, unless you have a nasal obstruction in which case you may use your mouth. Pay close attention to your breath leaving your chest and belly. Feel the air move through your passageways in your body as it finally leaves your nose.

3. **The following breaths are to be fifteen heartbeats on the inhale and fifteen heartbeats on the exhale.**

If you cannot pace your breath to fifteen heartbeats, do what you are comfortable with. Count silently inside your mind to the beat or rhythm of your heart. Therefore, your count may be slightly faster or slower than another person and may even vary from breath to breath depending on your heart rate. If you cannot feel your heart beat at first, count to what you think the rhythm might be. The point here is getting in touch with your body and the function of breath. This will take you to the next step of experiencing your soul more deeply and the presence of God.

When all is calm in your mind and emotions, which it will be after several passes of this technique, you are ready for the invocation. You have created equilibrium in your total energy by regulating your breath. This has thus regulated your *mental* and *emotional* fields, which has consequently regulated your *physical* body. Now you are ready for your *spiritual* energy to come in and align with the rest of your total being. Your *soul* or *spiritual energy* is very close to the experience of God's energy. We will first bring in a greater experience of your soul and then the presence of God.

4. **Ask your soul to completely come into your body so that you may more fully experience it. Be with this for ten to twenty minutes.**

As you do this, remain focused on your breath. Keep the rhythm of your breath going and invoke your soul. Your soul is already in your body but with this exercise you will experience your soul on greater and much deeper levels.

I will leave how you experience your soul to you. It may be *visually* with colors. You could *feel* tingling or vibrations rolling through your body such as a brush against your skin, hair standing up on end or a gentle blow of the wind against your body. It may also be subtle like a slightly warm feeling in one or more parts of your body. The idea is to eventually *feel* a fluid, water-type energy flowing through your field of energy and body. It may be a heavy feeling or light feeling. You might *hear* an inner voice or notice guiding thoughts come into your mind. You may even sense the hum of the energy as it fully enters your body. You will *know* when your soul comes into you because of the power you *feel*. It is analogous to confidence, grounded centeredness, as well as determination to go on and complete your life purpose.

5. Then bring God in.

I am God.

You may call on me or any name of God that you are comfortable with.

Believe It Is Possible To Become One With God. Or at least be open to God coming into your body and healing you.

6. Immediately you feel energy come over you.

You may experience this as a sense of peace or relaxation, comfort and things seeming just right. You have now opened up to the energy of God to come in to your body and heal you. This Is Possible. Accept It Is Happening.

7. This relaxed energy you feel will be followed by your breath changing as you allow God to direct your breath now, instead of focusing on it as you had previously. Experience this for ten minutes.

As you let go of your focus, you fall into a deep and open awareness of yourself that has no thoughts but rather intense or moderate feelings. As this happens, you may feel something similar to a wave or cushion of air pressing against your body. This is the power of the energy. When you feel this, know it is changing you forever and you will never be the same.

8. **You may ask God anything. Speak from your heart. Your intention at this point is to return your awareness to your inner child.**

The *inner child* is the *innocence* you were born with. It is not a thing but an experience of life. Ask God to take you into this and let go. This is not a space of the mind. It is a space of beingness. By *beingness* I mean specifically being with your experience in the moment without expectation or attachment to a particular outcome. It is *freedom* in its finest form. You simply *allow* whatever is to happen, to happen, knowing that where you go and what you experience is in God's hands now.

Surrender . . . give your control over to me that you have created to protect yourself from this world. Be present with the feelings. *Feel* the feelings; grounding into them will open you to their messages. I also ask you to remain *neutral* and do not judge to the best of your ability what comes in.

Many times people judge an experience as *wrong* or *bad*. Thus, they turn away from the experience or do not allow it to fully present itself in the first place.

By consciously asking God to show you truth and to provide you with who you really are and have been, you are setting up an opening that will allow whatever is to come up as memories, feelings, thoughts and visions to happen.

You are now ready to remember your *purity*. It might have been so long that you have forgotten altogether what it is like to be a child, so free, so uninhibited, fearless and innocent. There is of course a balance to all of these qualities. However please for now, give yourself permission to experience them without thought of how much or how little the balance should be. Let go completely of judgment and become a child again.

After accepting God into your body and energy field and asking God to help you experience your inner child, you may be immediately brought to a past childhood memory or feeling. When this happens, open your heart to the experiences that are shown to you. Be with them and take as long as you need to complete the exercise. Your breath will help to center you and bring you through to the next vision, feeling and memory. You may receive visions for hours of childhood memories that you forgot. You are reacquainting yourself with your past. This is important because your past is creating your present.

At some point you will want to have a total acceptance of every experience in your life. This is something to work towards. When you accept your total self including your past, present and potential future experiences, you are experiencing *soul-based living*. This, as mentioned previously, does not mean you have to agree with the experiences, just *accept* they happened and be *okay* with them. If you do not accept them, I will show you an exercise later that will help you to clear your personality thereby allowing you to accept your total self.

TIPS TO REDISCOVER YOUR INNER CHILD

Pay close attention to the following points when rediscovering your inner child. They will guide and comfort you through the process.

- If you do not have hours to spend delving into the montage of visions and feelings, dedicate *special sessions* as often as your schedule allows.

- Please keep a *journal* of your experiences. It will allow you to come back and get acquainted with your life and childhood.

- Your *breath* can help to open up your emotions and your emotions can take you further into your memories. Being present and accepting of your emotions as they swell from within you will also help.

- Emotions are one of the most challenging pieces of an experience to remember, especially if you were abused physically or verbally. Allow what comes up to move and *give the inner child a voice.*

- Since you chose to do this exercise and have given yourself enough time to get into this space, please make sure you also give yourself enough time to

play in this space. With no one around but you, you
may let your guard down completely and be spontaneous.

Do you notice how spontaneous children are? They do
what they feel in the moment. It isn't until they learn what
is right and what is wrong that their spontaneity dwindles.
Spontaneity is part of the passion of living; it is essential. If
you are inspired to play as a child please do so. This may
happen before you immerse yourself into the emotions and
thoughts you had as a child. To open yourself up to the experiences you have closed down, play with spontaneity.
These can include rolling around on your bed, going to the
kitchen and grabbing whatever you're inspired to eat, running outside and climbing a tree or skipping around the
neighborhood.

Kids love nature, especially animals, because of the natural
vibration that nature holds. Your innate, natural innocence
is synced to the vibration of nature, which is the heartbeat
of the Earth and the pulse of the Universe. Put another way,
the vibration or essence of nature is harmonized with your
soul. Most people pull themselves out of this harmonizing
vibration. Your soul and innocence will become more apparent as a result of harmonizing with this universal pulse.

If you have children play with them. Play ball and games,
make a fort or play other such activities that they may like.
Ask them what they would like to do. Really get involved
and look at the play from their perspective. For example if
you make a fort, please do your best to get into their energy

.

of what it feels like and what motivates them to make a fort. Play hide-and-go-seek. When you do, get in to the energy of what it feels like and what intrigues kids to play such a game. When you play with dolls and other toys, do your best to be aware of the experience children have as they play with them. Become like a child, intrigued with these simple pleasures. Climb a tree or a hill. Make a rope swing and feel the rush of flying around on it.

> ➤ For just a moment or hours, or as long as you can, dedicate yourself to this form of self-therapy. Let go of everything that seemed so important to you. Let go and have no responsibility except to play.

The more playdates you create with children, the more you will get to know the child space. Hence, you will be able to hold that consciousness in the rigid, common, expected day-to-day living of adults. Other adults will see your example of *freedom* and *innocence* and they will want the grace of living that you have obtained. They will see that the tight, rigid boxes that have confined them are not fun and do not bring them joy. Not only children but adults will benefit from your newfound passion for living . . . living from your innocence.

If you do not have children and are not able to be with kids, become a silly kid and play with yourself. Isn't it magnificent how kids can create their own worlds of imagination and play? Give it a shot! Relax and let go. Create an imaginary playmate and go on an adventure. Possibly you have an animal you can take to a park or natural setting, but if you don't go anyway and bring your imaginary friend. "But, why?" you may ask. By remembering your imagination and creative tools, you will not only remember your innocence but you will learn how to be a powerful manifester. The tools that children wield are the universal tools that govern creation and life. By remembering these tools, then learning how to effectively use them in your life, you will increase your wealth, joy and success manyfold.

THREE INNER CHILD ADVENTURE EXERCISES

1. If you're on the beach, you can imagine a *pirate ship* off in the distance coming. You must bury your treasure in the sand before the pirates make it ashore.

2. At a park, you can imagine you're in the *Amazon jungle* and there are natives around. Your pet jaguar, or other animal, is extremely friendly to you and protects you.

3. Lie down and close your eyes. Imagine you are lifted off on a magic carpet to the *golden city of the ancients*. There you meet beings of God that have mysterious messages for you. You are off on a mission of great importance.

As you can see, your adventures can go anywhere.

The point I am trying to make is that children live in their imagination and as they grow older it is greatly stripped away from most of them. Recreating your *imagination* is one of your greatest tools for self-mastery and embracing the ultimate sovereign power of your soul.

Simply play. Create playdates as often as you can, even if it's just yourself and your imaginary friends. What you will find is your imaginary friends may give you very helpful advice, as a form taken on by your spiritual guides.

Playing is one form of expressing your inner child and will open doors to remembering experiences when you were younger, if you had forgotten them. Whether you have forgotten them or not, everyone to some degree has forgotten the viewpoint of the child, the innocence I have previously talked about. So with that, let us delve into the child perspective, if you already haven't.

The natural *energy* of a child is one of mystery and intrigue. The greatest minds have created their inventions and philosophies from the perspective I'm talking about. This perspective includes humility, acceptance, love and intuition.

The questions children ask are necessary for them to see around the corners of life so they may comprehend this Physical Universe they were born into. The imbalance is in the adult viewpoint of what this Physical Universe is and how to live in it.

Children aren't asking how they can be like you. They are asking you, as a *role model*, how they can learn to be a balanced human being. Therefore you are in a position of authority over children. It is essential to put yourself in their shoes. Children trust their caretaker to provide adequate answers about how to live as a human. Still, children want to be their own person and develop into the human they came to Earth to be. If the balance is upheld between the child and caretaker, the child successfully develops their personality and completes their objective for their lifetime.

The most significant model for a person to follow is the model of the child. Let your inner child feel intrigued with whatever it is drawn to. As an adult, your interests may have been thwarted away from the basic pleasures of the child to more serious ventures like social stature, wealth, career gratification, intelligence or just simply how to survive by putting food on the table and gas in the car.

Whatever you have been focused on, please spend time each day to live freer in the newfound innocence of your inner child.

HUMAN CONNECTION EXERCISE

1. When you see a stranger, instead of looking away really connect with the person and be warm as if you already know them.

2. Even if you aren't dressed proper or looking just perfect, ask someone you have never met if they'd like to do something fun with you. You may call this a date or engagement. I call it a playdate. Use your intuition or ask your imaginary friend which person to ask out.

Let not your status, looks or background control your friendliness with others. Let your childlike innocence run your life and you will find yourself with more joy than you have known in a long time.

Popularity is a common motive for being one way with one person instead of how you might be with someone else. You may speak and act differently with your boss at work than with a friend. For the same reason you may be different with kids at school who are popular than with kids who are not popular.

Teach your children about *equality* and to treat everyone equally. They have learned otherwise from you and their surroundings. Learn once again with children what equality means and how to live it. Most would act differently with a bum on the street than with the president of your country. Why? Because of fear and judgment. Practice treating everyone the same right now—every human!

If you cannot be yourself around everyone, you are not *being real* and have a split personality. My emphasis is for you to have *one personality* that you are honored to show to the entire world, and if you are not, work on it and find out why. When you find out why, shift it and lower your guard that you have created to keep you safe in certain situations.

You Are Always Safe . . . Now . . . Forever More.

If someone is treating you unfairly as a result of you being yourself, you will want to stand in your truth and let them leave your life or realize that possibly your outlook needs to change about the situation. This is the great dilemma within companies, families and governments. There is a certain fakeness upheld to create an image of you that is false. Please rethink this.

Be *honest* with children. If you cannot be honest with children ask yourself why. You might say, "It is normal to lie and tell a story to children to keep them safe."

➤ What are you really keeping children safe from, the world or their perspective of you?

It is a mounting situation as families abuse drugs, cheat on each other, lie, steal, manipulate and physically, sexually, emotionally and mentally abuse each other. What will it take for you to take responsibility for yourself?

Children are your greatest indicators if you are living balanced or not. If you feel uncomfortable sharing something with your children there is something to explore. Children are the innocence that you must grow into. They are the salvation and no one sees it. Today's children are your best tool to change your life.

You can't hide from kids. It is crucial to know the mechanism of how children learn adults' beliefs. They learn how to be a human from you. There is *nothing* you can hide from children.

For instance, if you:

- Hide your life, children will grow up and learn to hide theirs.

- Hide your drug dependency, children will grow up learning to be dependent and hide their dependency.

- Tell kids one thing and do something else, they will learn to lie.

- Face your life and accept who you are, they will learn to accept themselves and be honest.

- Live from your soul, children will live from their souls.

- Love yourself, they will love themselves.

You Are Their Role Model. Who You Are, Your Children Will Become.

Also be especially conscious of who is caretaking for your children, for the caretaker will be the role model in your absence. The amount of time your kids spend with a caretaker (babysitter, relative, friend or teacher) will directly determine the influence the caretaker has on your kids. How your child views the caretaker is also important. If the child adores their caretaker then they will accept more beliefs about life from this person, whereas if the child rejects the caretaker the effects upon them will be less. However, regardless of the child's like or dislike of an adult, the child is accepting, to some degree, the adult's beliefs and that adult will surely influence their personality to some extent.

The Inner Child Meditation may prompt you to remember certain caretakers that you had as a child. It will also enable your subconscious to show you the root experience where you accepted your present beliefs. I will help you to find and change any beliefs that aren't supporting soul-based living. Please note that changing a life experience may require you to change several beliefs or a belief system to completely resolve the experience. For now remember whatever your mind reveals to you and be with the memories as they come up.

At this time you are allowing yourself to become, *energetically*, a child again. Thereupon, you may reveal and embrace your entire life and eventually, hopefully, you will live from the innocence that you were born with.

Another excellent way that you can get in touch with your inner child is to buy toys and do activities that you did as a child. This will open you to the energy that you had as a child. Do not be afraid to play with toys. Isn't it funny that if friends and family saw an adult playing with toys, it would be an awkward situation to say the least? Let this not stop you, but instead, turn into the child again and fill your shelves with some of your favorite childhood games and toys. The most significant part of this experience is to remember the *feelings* you had when you would play with the toys and how your *imagination* would take off into realms of the mysterious and mystical.

Most people have a *split personality* consisting of at least two parts. A split personality contains:

1. The child that has been muffled from speaking and feeling because of the trauma experienced as a child.

2. The adult that has muffled the child from speaking and feeling.

The second personality may start to develop as early as age six or sooner, depending on the conditioning that the parents imparted on the child. If this is the case, valuable stages of development were *colored*. This will result in a severely imbalanced perspective of the world, the self and relationships with others.

Again, allow the child in you to *speak up* and *feel*. Be with it and realize it is okay to embrace everything that you feel and think. It is easy to block the inner child from speaking and feeling with adult ideas and philosophy about what is acceptable and good, but please let all judgment go and give your inner child a voice to express itself.

As you make a space for your inner child to express itself through feeling, vision, voice and action, you will once again remember what it was like to be innocent and pure.

Chapter 10

THE CLEARING GAME

I will show you how to change your thoughts and emotions that have boxed in your innocence.

Each life experience has a belief or beliefs creating it. Each belief was accepted by your subconscious mind at some point. The point it was accepted is called the *root experience*, meaning the root or foundation of the belief.

By revealing where and from whom the belief was accepted, you can change the belief.

Changing the belief will change your life experience. Emotions are the result of beliefs. By changing your beliefs, you will change the experience of your emotions.

CHANGE YOUR BELIEFS TO CHANGE YOUR LIFE

Your *subconscious* is the *data storage space* of your mind that allows beliefs and programmed responses to be held. It is your hard drive, synonymous to a computer, storing information for retrieval and usage.

Most people are unaware of their subconscious programmed beliefs. There are many subconscious beliefs running in your mind at one time.

Below are examples of contrasting beliefs. These examples will help you to better understand your own beliefs. You may find that you experience some opposing beliefs simultaneously.

EXAMPLES OF BELIEFS

- I like myself *or* I dislike myself.

- I do trust myself and others *or* I don't trust myself and others.

- I express all of my emotions and thoughts *or* I don't express all of my emotions and thoughts.

- All of my emotions and thoughts are accepted *or* all of my emotions and thoughts are not accepted.

- I am beautiful *or* I am ugly.

- I can do anything *or* I cannot do anything.

- I am smart *or* I am stupid.

- Life is fun and easy *or* life is hard and troublesome.

- People will help me *or* people will hurt me.

- I am safe in the world *or* I am unsafe in the world.

- Alcohol and chemicals are not part of my life to take *or* alcohol and chemicals are part of my life to take.

- Smoking does not serve me *or* smoking does serve me.

- People love me the best they can *or* people should love me better.

- I am doing the best I can at my job *or* I am not doing well enough at my job.

- I accept my truth first and foremost over others' *or* I accept others' truth about me over my own.

- Love is for everyone *or* love is for some but not others.

- I do trust myself to succeed *or* I don't trust myself to succeed.

- Making money is easy *or* making money is hard.

- Living in the world is exciting and fun *or* living in the world is stressful and scary.

- God will speak to me *or* God will not speak to me.

- Miracles will happen to me *or* miracles will not happen to me.

- My life is a blessing *or* my life is a curse.

- I choose to understand and learn from others *or* I choose to blame others.

Each belief will give you a specific experience of life. A belief may cause an emotional or physical response. The response could be *chosen* or *instinctual.* By changing a belief you change your experience of life. The change could take many forms. The above list of beliefs shows you the myriad of experiences you can change in your life.

THE CLEARING GAME TECHNIQUE

There is an easy technique to *clear* subconscious beliefs, for good, so you can be free to experience life the way you want. You may call this technique *The Clearing Game.*

The name of this technique describes its purpose which is to clear limiting subconscious beliefs through play. The Clearing Game is a healing game meant to be fun as well as helpful.

Children will have imbalanced beliefs in their subconscious minds at the youngest of ages, so you will want to use the technique with them as well. We will use this technique along with The Five Accomplishments to clear anything undesired in the mind. This technique is best for children, as it is a *game* more than a *therapy session*. Many children can find it fun depending on how you present it to them.

The technique uses your ten percent *conscious mind* to guide you through a series of questions and answers. The answers are pulled from the usually inaccessible *subconscious mind* and are quickly looked at, then changed, so that the subconscious can be reprogrammed with new beliefs.

With this method you can also access your *intuition*, which helps you guide the session. The technique opens your subconscious mind and spiritual abilities. It uses a direct connection between your mind and the movement, or at least visualized movement, of your hand. The unstructured, intuitive movement of the participant's hand enables them to access and change subconscious beliefs. Many individuals have used this premise to shift and release stored emotions in the body and to change beliefs in the mind. Some cultures use dance to open the subconscious mind and intuition. Others have used writing or drawing to achieve the same result.

This technique is not something you think about. It is *spontaneous*, which is why it is so useful with children and to bring your inner child out.

You may use The Clearing Game with yourself or with another adult as a participant. I will show you how to use it to facilitate understanding and growth with children. This is the single most advanced way of helping kids presently in the world. Through using this technique with other modalities you have learned, you will have a great advantage in helping children.

Because The Clearing Game uses the movement of the hand you will find a rhythm to the experience. **As you and the child say something you move your hands.** You may move your hand with every word, sentence or breath. Also it could simply be to a rhythm of time like once a second or every few seconds. Clearly there is no wrong time interval for moving your hand. The technique works best if the hand moves at least with every concept or sentence. The movement of your hand can be from one place to another, from high to low or any other way you choose.

Allow your child's *imagination* **to run wild.** You and the participant can imagine picking something up from one pile and placing it in another pile. This brings out enthusiasm with the child and brings you into their world. **Be sure the movement is consistent,** not sporadic, as children can get sidetracked by the movement of their hand during a session. **The key is to use the moving hand as a focal point**, not necessarily to look at it, but as you move your hand your subconscious mind is opened and accessed. **The result is children share** things that they normally wouldn't share and they feel things they normally wouldn't feel. These include visions, thoughts and memories from any point in time.

Use *imaginary objects* to experience the session more as a *game*. By using such objects you would have a pile on one side of a table or the floor, pick them up and set them down onto another pile. With smaller imaginary objects you may hold them in one hand, pick them up with the other hand and lie them down onto the pile. **Both participants will move their hands the entire session.**

If a disability prevents you from moving your hand, simulate in your mind's eye the movement of your hand. Use your imagination to visualize picking objects up with your hand.

It is imperative to assure the child there is *no wrong way* to participate. Use the soul-based philosophy for your session where you are the observer without judgment.

There must be *freedom* with the session so the child feels comfortable. Focus is also essential.

The child may feel uncomfortable at first. **Explain it this way, "We are going to play a game and talk about things."** You will talk about either what just happened or a past experience. There may not be a particular motivation, per se, for using the technique in the moment other than to communicate with the child.

Children, at least in this world, will tend to feel uncomfortable speaking about their innermost feelings if adults haven't listened to them or have disregarded them previously. Please put your judgment aside and look at the child as well as your past efforts as a caretaker or teacher from the observer. You are to *remain an observer* and not get involved with the child's emotions and thoughts other than from a *neutral* standpoint. It is not your place to blame or prove your point. Instead try to comprehend and appreciate where the child is coming from. They have a reason for what they are saying or they wouldn't say it. Attempt to *learn* from what they are telling you. I know it can be challenging to hear your child say they don't feel loved or don't like things that you do. But Just Listen First. Use the list of soul-based qualities shown previously in this book to set the tone for your session.

> Do you know how amazing it is for a caretaker to simply listen to a child and the child feel heard?

Most often children are told what to do with little to no explanation or reason and unpermitted to question the adult.

The child is a person. The child is a soul. Most of all, children offer adults valuable lessons and insight, just as you offer it to them.

In the beginning of the session it is especially important to simply *listen* to the child to create an environment that the child can *trust* to be vulnerable in.

Most crucially during your session, **Never, Ever, use things a child shares with you in session against them in**

the future. Your special time with the child is where they are to feel safe and heard. If you use information against them and they no longer feel safe to share openly with you, then you will have closed a very important opportunity for them to open up in the future.

Be the *observer* and *listen*. Then you will begin to *understand* your child.

You may talk about something that just happened such as the child misbehaving or not doing their homework. In any case, I suggest you first *clear* yourself and shift your point of view to that of the *neutral observer*, if you are not already there. Really before any session or special talk with someone, it is crucial to come from the observer. This will allow God to come into you. Thus, you will be in alignment with whatever the child needs in the session.

God will come into the session and create the highest benefit for both of you. It may have been a long time since you were a child and you may have forgotten the child space. Because of this, **bring God in to give you insights about the child and situation.**

It may be challenging at first to participate with your child from the observer perspective because you have, for the life of the child, been the authority figure. Now you are simply an ear for the child to vent to and share their innermost feelings and thoughts. Please, with emphasis:

Please, Do Not Judge What They Share.

Judging them will create mistrust towards you in their most vulnerable space, something that will not benefit you. If you cannot stay detached and remain the observer, it is much better to stop the session and pick it up another time or have someone else facilitate the child.

Thank you for your patience with children in attempting to understand them and make their lives a little easier.

You may easily use The Clearing Game technique to comprehend the real motivation of why a child disobeyed rules or was disrespectful. This can be for a myriad of reasons. **The *root* of almost every action is the desire to love and be loved.** This means *feeling accepted.* Beyond this motivation, a perceived imbalanced action may be the result of a simple misunderstanding.

As you do sessions with a child keep a *journal* of everything they express to you, so you can have a reference for future sessions and the progress of their development.

Chapter 11

CREATING CLEAR COMMUNICATION

I will show you how to recognize and balance disharmony in the way children and adults communicate.

How children learn to express themselves and interpret their life experiences will directly show in their behavior. Therefore, if you show your child how to accurately, or rather clearly, express their experiences, they will show balanced behavior that is more predictable.

If you have a history of teaching children unbalanced ways to communicate, learn with them how to communicate clearly.

INTUITIVE COMMUNICATION

INTUITIVE INNER SEEING QUALITY

When you dream or daydream and receive *visions* in your mind, you are using your intuitive inner seeing quality. This quality is also used to see nonphysical energy such as auras, energy fields and spirits.

INTUITIVE INNER FEELING QUALITY

Gut feelings, as many have called them, originate usually as a *sense* to do something or not do something. Gut feelings are your intuitive inner feeling quality. Many have used this form of intuition to feel someone out and know if they are a person to associate with or not. Others have felt into situations to determine if the experience is for their highest benefit. Many great discoveries have been revealed from gut feelings. Such discoveries might include archeological digs, mathematical theorems and technological advancements where the discoverer had a hunch that led them to the perfect solution.

Intuitive feelings tell children whether they are safe to express themselves or not. Children learn to feel into others so they may know when to share and when not to. Adults have created proper times to share and improper times. Instead of memorizing every situation that may come up and how to respond according to what the adult deems as *right* or *wrong*, the child learns to feel into it with their intuition.

This is not natural. It is a living mechanism brought about by the adult's conditional acceptance of the child.

INTUITIVE INNER HEARING QUALITY

The intuitive inner hearing quality is responsible for intuitive *thoughts* coming into the mind or even *voices*. Many of today's children hear voices as intuition and it concerns adults. There is nothing to be concerned about. The voices or thoughts children experience are more than likely the child's spiritual guides or their own intuition.

IMAGINARY FRIENDS

Sometimes the child has created an actual imaginary friend. It can be someone the child plays and creates with or a living mechanism. More than likely perceiving an imaginary friend is not detrimental to the child.

If the child has created an imaginary friend as a living mechanism, which will take understanding on your part, you may use The Clearing Game to explore why the child has created it and balance the living mechanism.

In more cases than not it is extremely beneficial to have an imaginary friend. The way you would *learn* about the child's imaginary friend is to just ask questions and *listen*. Do not judge or tell them how to experience their friend. The Clearing Game is a *discovery game* to allow you to learn more about yourself and others.

If you find the root cause of why they created an imaginary friend is a living mechanism and introduce your support based on your findings, the need for the living mechanism will go away. It is not something you need to tell them to stop playing with. Attention does not need to be brought to it other than for you to *learn about it* and *support them.*

Children would love to share about their creations but find many times adults don't accept them and discount them. Please *embrace* their imagination. Really desire to *appreciate* and *understand* their world. Then, you have created a bridge which allows you into their world so that you can help them. You live in a beautiful world, especially when seen through the eyes of a child. Learn, explore and experience your innocence.

INTUITIVE INNER KNOWING QUALITY

The intuitive inner knowing quality is an *instant experience* of information without thought. It can be part of the spontaneity children have. Children will know things without any real explanation. This comes from the knowing quality.

Any other nonphysical experiences perceived by a child will more than likely fall under these four qualities, or at least are translated with them.

In order to comprehend the ineffable experiences of their four qualities, children will ask many questions. This makes for a lot of information being expressed from within the child including visions, thoughts and feelings. This is one motivation why children like to talk a lot. In the process of questioning and talking, they are creating an interface between their interpretations and expressions of their physical and nonphysical experiences. This *interface* is called communication as you know it. *Communication* is therefore how you express your interpretation of your life experience.

Realizing that what a child expresses on the outside is more than likely not representing the child's true experience on the inside gives you a bird's eye view into why you don't understand the child's behavior. In retrospect you may find that the child does not understand your behavior. By you and the child understanding each other, many doors will open and your relationship with the child will be deepened. Really you are on a journey back to the *clear expression* of your *inner experience* with the world. Journey this together with your family, friends, colleagues and others. It will be the one thing, more than anything, which will bring harmony and success to any situation.

Aligning your inner experience of life with your outer expression of that experience will, in fact, eliminate all confusion. The way you express your experiences of life determines how much or little others will understand you and you them. By creating clarity with yourself, you will have clarity in understanding others and will therefore be able to benefit everyone you meet.

The point of The Clearing Game session is to create a *safe* environment where you and the child may *let your guard down* and learn about each other. To do this, first listen to the child and then work through the confusion either on your part or theirs. Usually it is both sides that require clarity.

This world can turn the problem of miscommunication around rather quickly. Learn and then teach your children how to align their inner experience with their outer communication of it. Then the child's inner feelings and thoughts will match up with their words and actions. There will be a true marriage of the child's inner experience with their outer expressions. In doing so, your planet will experience truth.

Love yourself enough to really look at this. Then decide if you want to continue on the road you have walked or choose the easier road, the freer road, the road which shares love abundantly and is clear of obstacles.

Humanity has created such trouble for itself by removing clear, easy ways of expression and replacing them with some of the most complex, confusing ways to communicate.

Let go of the old and call out for a change in your homes and schools, as well as in your companies and governments. Live free and clear to express the beautiful soul that you are and shine your light to the world. Thank you for your interest in supporting children to express their soul's clear, loving nature! Please be proud of your bravery for trying something new. When you triumph and see a free world in peace and harmony, you will indeed celebrate. Blessings . . . my child.

EXERCISES TO CLEARLY COMMUNICATE

The following exercises will enable you to reflect, reveal and transform any unclear, imbalanced communication and assist children to do the same. Please follow along with the exercises by writing in your *journal*.

CHILDHOOD COMMUNICATION EXERCISE

1. Go back in time to the first memory you have of being around another child, whether it is your brother or sister, a friend at school or stranger.

    Possibly you can't remember being around other children when you were younger so remember as far back as you can.

2. How old were you? Where was it? What were you doing?

3. Get a vivid, real experience of the memory and listen to what you were attempting to express from your inner experience. It could have been fun, joy, anger, sadness, jealousy or even contentment.

4. How did you express your inner experience to the child you were with? Was your experience on the inside similar to what you expressed physically to the child?

5. Observe and describe how you communicated. Did you express your feelings and thoughts clearly or unclearly? If you expressed them unclearly, why?

6. Explore several more examples from that time period.

PARENT-CHILD COMMUNICATION EXERCISE

1. Look at your parents from the standpoint of when you were a child.

2. How did they communicate with you? Was it a clear or unclear expression? Did they do what they said? Did they say what they meant?

3. Could they express their innermost feelings and thoughts with each other and you?

4. Did they allow you to express your innermost feelings and thoughts, or did you have to learn to filter certain things that they didn't want to hear or see?

   For instance, it is incredibly common for an adult to become uncomfortable when a child cries. Was this true with your parents?

5. Do you become uncomfortable around children who cry?

Crying is as *natural* as eating. It is an expression of the inner experience. If you block a child from crying you are blocking their expression in more ways than you realize. A child does not resort to crying unless there is a storehouse of emotional energy. If there is that much emotional energy it needs to go somewhere. When you block a child from crying the emotional energy goes straight into their physical body. Consequently, it begins to cause disease in the body. It also disrupts their emotional and mental energies. If the release of emotional energy has been blocked, it is important for the block to be cleared.

If you are uncomfortable with children who cry, you learned it somewhere and you must change the belief creating your discomfort for both your well-being and theirs.

COMMUNICATING DISAGREEMENT EXERCISE

1. Were you allowed to disagree with your parents or teachers?

   This probably sounds absurd to many adults, to allow a child to disagree with them.

2. Do you get uncomfortable if a child disagrees with you?

If you were not allowed to disagree with adults when you were a child and if you find yourself uncomfortable today when a child disagrees with you, change the belief creating it so you are comfortable with disagreement. Children who are blocked from disagreeing learn to manifest anger. Disempowering beliefs and behaviors develop as a result of blocking their ability to disagree.

For instance, you might notice that the confidence level of a child drops significantly when they are not allowed to disagree. Their self-esteem is affected and they begin to doubt themselves. The detrimental effect on a child depends on how severe the punishment is for disagreeing.

A child is a soul in a human body and deserves *respect*, even though this world has built family values on disrespecting children in many cases.

RESPECTING CHILDREN EXERCISE

1. Do you really respect children as you do an adult? Are your ears just as interested in what they have to say as your spouse or mentor that you would look up to for advice?

Children have more to teach you about living a balanced life than most adults. Children are your greatest gift to knowing how to create peace and harmony in the world.

Please Respect Children As You Respect Any Mature Adult.

You, as an adult, are still an authority figure. Because of your experiences in life and lessons you've learned, you have much to teach them and you will. Just as well, they have much to teach you. Please be aware of the balance of *guiding* them with your authority and *allowing* them to mature into an autonomous human being. There is a balance. It will take you time to learn the balance with children. Through reading this book you will learn the impactful tools that are available to you. The destiny of this planet is in your hands as you shape and form today's children.

BODY LANGUAGE ALLOWANCE EXERCISE

1. Were you allowed to show expression on your face or did your caretakers punish you for it?

It is very common for a caretaker to criticize a child for a frown or an angry look; some adults punish kids for laughing. It's uncomfortable for an adult to be around a child that shows expression if the adult learned it was a *bad* thing to do and is incapable of doing it themselves, or at least looks down on themselves when they do it.

2. Are you uncomfortable when children frown? Do you think something is wrong?

Can I be completely forthcoming with you? Stop judging emotions and thoughts. Stop judging actions. Stop judging period and learn unconditional acceptance, which is *True Love.*

Instead of *judging* the way children express themselves attempt to *learn* what is beneath their communication. Show interest in what they are really meaning and saying with their expressions. Use your intuition and bring intuitive understanding into every relationship in your life.

Do you even care what children are really trying to express? If so, take time to understand them. It is worth it to you and them. Just because you don't have the patience to spend time with a child to comprehend what they really want you to know is not their fault. Children Take Time.

If you are a parent, you have a responsibility under universal laws to spend time with your child to ensure they will properly complete all stages of development to become a capable, balanced human being. If you do not *choose* to take on this responsibility find a caretaker that will and do not have any more babies, please.

The world is filled with children that are not wanted by their parents. You would be surprised how many adults you know personally that feel their children inconvenience them. Do you? If you do it is not abnormal. It is exceptionally common in this world, and you wonder why children are crying out for love and help.

The inconvenience parents feel with their children is a major dysfunction in the collective consciousness of Earth. Many parents would say, "Isn't it normal to feel put out and inconvenienced by kids." Many teachers would say their students frustrate them and inconvenience them. It is easy to *blame* children.

COMMUNICATING RESPONSIBLY EXERCISE

1. When you were a child, did your parents blame you?

2. Do they still blame you?

3. How does that make you feel? Honestly, *be real* with yourself. How you feel about being blamed is incredibly similar to how children feel when you blame them. There is no shame in admitting your imbalances. It is graceful. Can you do it?

4. Can you admit your imbalances without blaming yourself or others? If you can, you are beginning to comprehend soul-based living.

Children know soul-based living until you teach them otherwise. It is like asking a fish to live out of water on the land. It's very foreign to the fish. Maybe the fish dies in the process. This is an extreme metaphor showing you the space you take children from. Still the metaphor is needed. Children feel like you are taking them out of a great place they love called *soul-based living* and forcing them into a scary, deadly place called *ego-based living*.

It is not their choice to leave the space of the soul. It is forced upon them by you. If you are part of the very small percentage that has not done this, congratulations; you are an example for the entire world. But if you are part of the majority of people on this planet, please take responsibility for your imbalances and balance them. I am showing you how to balance yourself. Just being open to self-help tools is a great accomplishment in itself. Be proud of yourself for looking into alternative ways to live and coexist with children.

I hope you are *keeping a journal* for the answers to all of the questions I have been asking you. The questions help you to know yourself and your children. If you are a parent, your children more than likely picked up most of their beliefs from you and the other parental figure. You will be able to use The Clearing Game on yourself to understand and change your subconscious beliefs, as well as children's.

Chapter 12

FIVE ACCOMPLISHMENTS TO BECOMING ONE WITH YOUR SOUL

I will speak about how to use The Clearing Game with a process called *The Five Accomplishments*. The Five Accomplishments are five steps to becoming one with your soul and living from unconditional love, since the true expression of your soul is unconditional love.

The Clearing Game and The Five Accomplishments will be tailored for children. However, this book is not only for children but also to heal your inner child. Therefore, anyone can benefit from the perspective I am sharing.

A newborn child is living in rhythm with the Earth and nature. If allowed to develop naturally, an infant will become a child, then an adolescent and eventually grow into an adult living from their soul. In a balanced world there would be no need for The Five Accomplishments because their goal is to help you live from the soul-based perspective, and this would already be happening naturally in a balanced world. But this world is not balanced. Therefore, even children need The Five Accomplishments. Children can become unbalanced as soon as birth, and even while in the mother's womb their consciousness is affected.

Use The Five Accomplishments sequentially starting with accomplishment one and ending with five.

THE FIVE ACCOMPLISHMENTS

1. Get Grounded

2. Get Real with Your Life

3. Get Real with Your Inner World

4. Get Real with God

5. Initiation of the Soul

Chapter 13

ACCOMPLISHMENT ONE: GET GROUNDED

B eing *grounded* holds precedence above any other need you have, other than basic survival needs such as eating, sleeping and drinking water. This means before you begin a session with yourself or a child, check to make sure you are both grounded.

Why is it so important you may ask? Why is it more important than even healing yourself or overcoming obstacles in your life? Why does it hold a greater significance than success or accomplishments of any other kind? It is the one thing that may keep you from the need to return to this planet again. Let me explain.

Being *grounded* means you are *present* for your Earth experience. If you are ungrounded there is no reason for you to be here physically, for you are not present for your experiences anyway. The fact is that most people on Earth are not totally grounded for their Earth experience. Consequently, souls need to come back to Earth to repeat experiences they missed in previous lifetimes as a result of being ungrounded.

To the degree you are present for your experience is directly proportionate to how much of your experience your soul will choose to take back with it after your body dies and your soul crosses over to the Nonphysical Universe. It is analogous to someone who does not show up to their job and therefore does not receive compensation. If you are not present at your job to accomplish your tasks, there is no time counted towards your compensation. If you aren't present for your job on Earth, which is to be present for all your experiences mentally, emotionally, physically and spiritually, the experiences you were not present for do not count.

Can this really be true? Yes, it is fact.

My purpose with you right now is to impart the necessity to get your children grounded. Your responsibility to this world is to take care of the youth.

1. First, get grounded.

2. Then, ground children.

There was a time, several hundred thousand years ago, when children grew up fully knowing the power and intelligence of their soul. Without this valuable gift of awareness, one feels lost. Kids must recognize their power. Instead you, as a people, are taking their power away.

One way you take away children's power is by force-feeding drugs and toxins into their little bodies. This growing epidemic is numbing children with drugs, as well as ignorantly feeding them food with chemicals. These substances unground children in the worst way. Anything that goes into a child's body which is not *organic* and *neutral* to their system is violating universal laws, except when their life is threatened. Embrace a new way. The choice is yours.

I will spend a significant amount of time sharing information with you about how to get kids grounded. In order to ground someone—you need to be grounded. Be open to grounding yourself, for if you are not, the next four accomplishments won't be very effective.

Allow me to take you through an exercise to completely ground you, if you aren't grounded already. You'll ground your consciousness into your total physical experience:

- Physically (body)

- Emotionally (emotions)

- Mentally (mind)

- Spiritually (intuition)

FEET GROUNDING EXERCISE

1. **Start by taking three deep breaths from your stomach.** When you release each breath, do it quickly, blowing the air rather powerfully all the way down to your feet.

2. **Again, take three deep breaths.** On each exhale, blow all of your air powerfully down to the floor.

3. **Open your eyes and count to three as you breathe in.** As you do, open your arms as if you are about to hug someone.

4. **Then, exhale and hug yourself.** Squeeze tight as you exhale your air, blowing it to the floor.

5. **If you do not *feel* totally *solid* in your feet, do the first part of the exercise again.**

   This time focus on your feet the entire time. Actually *feel* your feet in your socks or on the floor. *Feel* where they are and what they are doing. Your intention is to bring your energy into your feet.

6. **When you feel you are solid and grounded into your feet, proceed to the next steps.**

7. **While keeping your eyes open, *imagine* ten stairs leading down through the floor . . . just pretend.**

8. **Take a *slow* breath with each step you take down the staircase.** Focus on how your feet *feel* the entire time. Start with your left foot and breathe. Be aware that with each step you go down, you become more *relaxed* and grounded. Really feel the heavy relaxation.

9. **Let go and *surrender* to God.**

10. ***Imagine* yourself wearing comfortable clothes . . . relaxed . . . in warm, shallow, clear, beautiful water.** It is warm out. Float on your back or swim around.

11. **Pay attention to your feet and how they *feel* the entire time.** *Feel* your physical feet as your imagination unfolds. You are safe and comfortable in this vision.

12. **Now you are totally grounded. You can trust it.**

If you feel the need for additional grounding, use the Inner Child Meditation illustrated previously in this book, with your eyes open, as you remain aware of your feet.

Feel the heaviness in your feet and *allow* God to come into you. Ask God To Ground You Even More.

Check to see if your child is also grounded.

You cannot trust the accuracy of checking someone else unless you are grounded first. Also if you are ungrounded, it can be harder to get them grounded.

The natural space of a person's consciousness is to be totally grounded in their physical experience. If one is not grounded they will energetically pull on others who are grounded in an attempt to pull themselves in. If you are around someone who is ungrounded they will pull on your energy. If you are ungrounded you will pull on theirs. This is why you may feel drained around certain people. If you do not have a total command of your energies and someone is ungrounded, they will pull on your energies. It will be uncomfortable, possibly to the point that you will need to rest. Kids are no exception.

Many kids today are ungrounded and parents feel the effects of it. They probably learned it from you or it occurred because of chemicals in their body from food and drugs, as well as environmental factors such as pollution and too much sun. Energetic pollution such as *EM fields* or electromagnetic fields may also affect them. EM fields include microwaves from cordless phones and mobile phone towers. Also particular lighting can cause disturbances in your health. This is common in school classrooms and businesses when fluorescent lighting is used.

The most helpful way to discern if you are grounded is to be aware of how you *feel*.

BODY GROUNDING CHECK-IN

1. Do you *feel* refreshed and heavy as if you just woke up from a long nap or do you *feel* a little spacey with thoughts running through your mind?

2. Do you literally FEEL your body or do you just THINK you feel your body?

   If you are in touch with your body and you can describe how the different parts of your body *feel*, there is a better chance that you are grounded.

Another way to check if you are grounded is to use your intuition.

INTUITIVE GROUNDING CHECK-IN

1. Intuitively *see*, *feel* or *know* exactly where and how far into the body your consciousness is grounded.

2. You may also ask spirit to give you an answer intuitively in your *mind*.

Ideally you want one's energies grounded all the way into their toes and even beyond several inches. One's consciousness can be imagined as a flowing, fluid energy. You must be grounded to be certain your intuition is accurate. If you are ungrounded the information you get intuitively may not be accurate. Therefore, using the Intuitive Grounding Check-In Exercise along with the Body Grounding Check-In Exercise will be a more accurate way to discern one's grounded state of being.

When your consciousness is out of its natural physical space and off in other spaces, you can pick up other energies from people, places and things. Many have mistaken people as being possessed or labeled them with mental and emotional illnesses, when in fact their ungrounded consciousness created the experience.

When you decide consciously or subconsciously that you do not want to be present for your life experience, your awareness leaves its natural space. When you leave this natural, balanced operating space you have no control over your energies, and most of all it kills you.

People who are ungrounded accelerate their aging process. If something is not sustaining your life with sustenance it is killing you. Most people in the world are ungrounded and therefore are perpetuating their aging process. When you are ungrounded, you will immediately or over time develop physical, mental and emotional imbalances or illnesses. You will also have spiritual distortions.

Being grounded is essential for your soul to get its experiences and communicate with you. Many are not fulfilling their life destiny and feel lost or confused as a result of being ungrounded.

Numerous factors contribute to why a person may become ungrounded. Let us explore some of them in detail.

Your body has a specific chemistry. If you alter your chemistry too much, it can unground you or be a struggle to remain grounded. The human body has a fragile balance that if upheld can create longevity. There are several key aspects to this balance.

The pH of your body is one factor. Your pH must be above 7.25 to avoid creating disease in the body. You may attain this by eating neutral foods which include anything occurring naturally in nature with no processing, heating or treating of any kind. When humans first lived on this planet they ate raw fish and plant life mostly. It wasn't until the human became a total land dweller that they started killing other types of animals and cooking them along with plant life.

Later in the evolutionary ladder of humans, within the last one hundred and fifty years, a drastic change in the preparing and processing of food arose. Humans have created ways of preserving food and creating appeal to the eye and tongue that affects the health of people. Now many foods are eaten with little to no nutrition and are made solely of processed artificial ingredients. This is in total violation of universal laws under self-love, the love you have for yourself and your body. Please look at this and change it at once.

Today's food plays a major factor in the epidemic of ADD and ADHD, among other classified diseases slapped on children, and adults for that matter. If you want to help your children, return to a natural way of preparing and eating food with as little processing and preservation as possible.

Consuming any manmade chemical is violating universal laws unless it is to preserve life, as when faced with a life threatening imbalance. But even then, you must be very careful not to use a chemical to *fix* the issue for it cannot. Most imbalances are rooted in beliefs accepted somewhere in one's life. Ideally the chemical would be used to help balance the body, mind and emotions while you work on the *real* issue. The only time exceptions may be made is when one's life is threatened and even then only under certain circumstances. The core belief or beliefs creating a life threatening illness must be addressed. A life threatening illness is one that will cause you to die if you do not quickly act.

I want to be clear. Almost any imbalance can be corrected with just the power of your mind and God. Your healing potential is far beyond what any human uses in today's world. Even the most capable healers are scratching the surface of the human capability to heal.

Do you realize the magnitude of degeneration the planet and human species is enduring from meaningless chemical processing to create your way of life? You are at a point of no return with the environment. Now prepare for what is coming and blunt the degree of catastrophe it will have on your lives.

All of these changes in lifestyle have helped unground humans, especially children. Harmful chemicals are in the soil. They are in the air. They are in your drinking water. They are even in the very foods, drugs and supplements that you consider healthy. You are killing yourselves and you think you're saving yourselves because of your capability to out-live your ancestors who died at a much younger age. Yes, it is true your ancestors died at a much younger age, but times were much different then and times are much different now.

It is more valuable for your soul to spend fewer years on Earth and gain more experiences, than to spend more years gaining fewer experiences. Gaining experiences is the reason you are alive. You will only gain them if you are grounded.

You teach children that technological and economic growth is more important than the health of your body and planet. By doing this, you will endure the consequences. To stop global warming, place your priorities in different directions. The fact is your influence on the world has destroyed many ecosystems already. This affects the ability of your soul to come back to Earth.

Your kids feel the effects of your actions. They are growing up with chemicals in their bodies at exceptionally young ages, before they are even born. This adds to increased cases of ADD, ADHD and other notable conditions. This causes you, as adults and professionals, to increase the chemicals put into their bodies by administering drugs to them. You may believe chemicals help them but they only mask the real causes which are primarily your ignorance and negligence.

You are treating children for their attention disorders so you don't have to pay attention to them. Think about it. Whether you don't have time or won't make time to pay attention to kids, you are violating universal laws. You are responsible for a child that is in your care, and biological parents have an even greater responsibility to their children. Wake up to the real world. It starts by getting grounded.

Love Children. Show them the respect they deserve by giving them time to be heard and understood. Many caretakers won't pay attention to kids because they are distracted by their own struggle with everyday life, others simply don't want to listen. Adults may feel jealous because they do not feel heard. This reflects how they treat their children. It is a widespread, growing epidemic as America and other world powers develop in strength and wealth. They continue to focus on materialistic gain rather than personal growth and creating peace.

Children tend to get distracted easily. Do you know why? There is so much going on in the world that they intend to learn. It overwhelms them. Be an advisor for what they are to pay attention to and what they are to let go of. Training them to be independent of you is the best solution. For now it is okay to give them direct advice as a step towards being self-empowered with their own answers.

➢ Children need a role model. Do you volunteer? If you do volunteer you have a great responsibility.

ADULT STRENGTHS AND LIMITATIONS EXERCISE

1. Make a list of your strengths, things that *feel comfortable*.

2. Make a list of your limitations, things that *feel uncomfortable*.

This will give you a *real* look at who you are. Things you are comfortable with you are more inclined to do and teach. Whereas things you are uncomfortable with you are less inclined to do and teach. If you know your strengths and limitations, you have a step forward beyond the average person. We will look at the child from this perspective.

CHILD STRENGTHS AND LIMITATIONS EXERCISE

1. Make a list with the child by asking them what they feel are their strengths, the things that make them *feel comfortable*.

2. Make a list of the things that the child identifies as making them *feel uncomfortable*, their limitations.

These lists are going to be your compass as you guide them in their best direction. In a balanced world it is imperative to guide them until the child is about ten years old. At ten they can make wise decisions based on their life experiences. However in this world, you may need to guide them until they are in their late teens and even twenties.

Understand your relationship to what you are teaching them. If you have no background in, say, dance and they are to learn dance as part of their purpose, research dance and the best way for them to learn it. Keep track of their development consistently. On a week-to-week or even day-to-day basis check in with their spiritual guides and yours for the best solution to their problems and life direction. Until they can make responsible choices on their own you are their physical guide; this is a great privilege. Many mentors or caretakers are bothered by the position of *guide* that they hold. It is a great honor to guide someone either as a human in the Physical Universe or as a spirit in the Non-physical Universe.

Base your intention to guide children on showing them how to guide themselves. Allow them to make some decisions on their own little by little; then, they may see how responsibility and consequence works from the process of decision making. This gives them a solid, real example of the universal law of free will. Share with them that you will not always be there to guide them as you have. At some point they will guide themselves, so it is necessary for them to learn how to do this.

SOUL-BASED DECISION MAKING

1. *Allow* them to make decisions and be responsible for their decisions.

2. *Explain* that their decisions may not always work out the way they planned.

3. *Evaluate* the outcome of their decisions. Show them step-by-step how their decision produced the outcome, so in the future they can make wiser decisions based on the lessons of their previous ones.

4. Do not judge them or make them feel guilty for decisions they make. Instead, *instill confidence* in them to

continue making decisions and to not be afraid of the decision-making process, despite challenges and inconveniences resulting from their decisions.

A significant lesson to share with your children is that they cannot mess up, no matter what. Be there to observe with them their actions and show them alternatives for next time. When a similar situation comes up in the future they will be wiser. As a result, they will evolve in life instead of staying stagnant as many people do.

Children's beliefs tend to bend in the direction of parent's beliefs. Therefore, change your perspective if you want your child's perspective to change. If your child is expressing unbeneficial behavior, look at this and act accordingly by changing the way you see the world and relate with your child. The child's unbeneficial behavior is mostly caused by distancing between the parents and child. Parents tend to create distance between them and their child due to their career or own issues at hand. Even so, a parent needs to take full responsibility for how a child behaves.

Each child has a unique personality with a unique soul.

If the child's personality is acting in a way that violates universal laws, the child learned it from another human and that person was likely their caretaker. If you do not want to continue handing down generational beliefs, please look at yourself and change yourself first. This is to be accomplished with the five steps I am outlining as The Five Accomplishments.

THE SOUL AND THE PERSONALITY

Your soul is one aspect of your awareness. It is usually experienced as dormant, so to speak, until the personality is clear enough to allow access to the soul. Until that point, the soul is not actively interacting with the Physical Universe since the personality is blocking it. The eternal soul created the personality to get a physical experience. Your personality consists of your physical, emotional, mental and spiritual energies.

Your soul is an observer. When you participate from the observer, soul-based perspective, you are living from the consciousness of your soul, to some degree or another. The degree to which you actually live from your soul's viewpoint depends on how clear your personality is to allow your soul's expression, which is unconditional love, to emanate in everything you do. Your soul is an energy that you, as a personality, do not control. However if your personality chooses to allow your soul to interact, it will. Thereupon, your soul may interact more actively with your experience. This interaction occurs to the degree you give your personality's wants and desires over to your soul. It is a fine balance that one masters after years of clearing work. The subconscious beliefs instituted in this world as a *normal* way of living are mostly dysfunctional and lead the personality away from a direct experience with the soul.

Again, your personality is an energy that you do have total control over. Your soul is an energy that you, as a personal-

ity, do not have control over, other than to ask it to participate and guide you.

The soul will not violate any universal laws unless the violation is accepted by a nonphysical soul council or God.
You as the personality would normally be unaware of such
an exception of standard practice.   .

Your soul will always choose to be grounded in your body.
Your personality or consciousness has a choice to be
grounded or ungrounded in your body. This means you
may take the energy of your personality into a space outside, or other than, your natural, grounded state of being.
This will make more sense as I go on.

You may be uncomfortable in a situation and not accept it
physically, mentally, emotionally or spiritually. If you do
not accept an aspect of your Earth experience, you will unground the energies of your personality. You will in essence be saying, "I do not accept my experience and do not
choose to be present for it."

Being Grounded Is Being Present And Unconditionally
Accepting Your Earth Experience.

The point above is fundamental for subsequent steps of The
Five Accomplishments to be used effectively. Getting
grounded requires you to rethink judgment altogether, including what you judge as *bad* and what you judge as *good*,
as well as what you judge as *wrong* and what you judge as
right. Remember the soul-based perspective has no judg-

ment, no proving, no blaming and no reason to choose sides. There is only *one side*, we are all in this together and everyone is doing the best they can. Everyone is respected, even if you disagree with another's point of view.

Presently children are mostly raised and taught from the ego-based perspective. This perspective of separation and judgment is extremely uncomfortable for them at first and they resist it. Eventually children that learn this perspective begin to judge and create separation. When you separate yourself from something, you literally divide your perspective. This is where duality comes in, another word for ego-based living. As you divide yourself from the rest of the world through judgment, you are dividing yourself from yourself under the law of oneness.

Let me illustrate this on a practical level with an exercise.

EGO-BASED JUDGMENT EXERCISE

1. Think to a time when you judged someone based on how they dressed, what they looked or sounded like, their religion or ethnicity or their beliefs. How did you feel when you did this?

2. Recall a time when anger was triggered from your judgment. Not simply a disagreement. An actual judgment where you wanted them to be different or see things like you because you felt you were *right* and they were *wrong*. How did you feel?

You felt totally separated. In fact, you did not even want to be *one* with them. You wanted to be *separate* from them. Think about this. What is this example telling you? You were not distancing yourself from them and their beliefs; you were distancing yourself from yourself. Something inside of you that you didn't like was reflected back to you from them. If you were not accepted as a child, at some point you may have agreed with those who judged you. Consequently, you began judging yourself. Since you accepted their belief or story about life it has played out in your life. Most people judge. Thus, there is work to be done. The only way to get completely grounded is to accept yourself, every aspect of your total being, and to stop judging.

Be an example of self-love for your children by raising them under universal laws and beliefs that will benefit them in life. Create your first intention to be completely grounded.

If children learn to be ungrounded they will miss their Earth experience. If this occurs, unless they do significant work on themselves as you are doing by reading this book and choosing to change your perspective, they will pass it on to you when you return for your next lifetime. Children will be future leaders and parents. Therefore, the generational beliefs of conditional acceptance and being ungrounded may haunt you for eons. Decide the generational cycle will stop today. Change now. Do not wait. Take responsibility for your life and children. But most importantly, take responsibility for the future lifetimes of your soul. Teach this world how to ground and be present.

The degree to which you are ungrounded for your life experiences is the degree to which your soul will not use those experiences for its overall destiny. In other words if you are fifty percent ungrounded, your soul will take back with it fifty percent of its experiences. This means you will return again and again to revisit previous experiences you have already been through but were not present to receive. Save your soul lifetimes of experiences by grounding. Teach the world. Tell everyone you know. The greatest gift you may give someone is to have their experiences count by showing them how to be grounded. Thank you for recognizing the significance of this universal law. You violate universal laws each time you unground your consciousness. For someone to actually choose to unground is in total contradiction of why you are living.

Many people spend time in ungrounded spaces of experience and call them spiritual or religious, supernatural or psychic. Many believe they must escape their humanness to connect with God. They believe that not being emotional or egotistical is how God will hear and answer them. Some even believe they must escape aspects of themselves for God to accept and love them. God Is With You Now . . . as you read these words. God is with you in your most judgmental of moments. When you feel completely alone the Divine is with you. Your job is to be present with all of your emotions, thoughts and actions. Escaping egotistical thoughts and uncomfortable feelings will only prolong the inevitable: you will need to face them and accept them at some point.

When you create separation with parts of yourself, you create the experience of separation with God, spirits and your soul. Do not attempt to live up to high religious or spiritual ideals at the cost of escaping reality. Work towards them. Take the ideas at a pace that works for you. This includes the essence of this book. As straightforward as my stance may be, please know there will be growing pains to reach these goals. There will be steps. Stay in your proper grounded experience every step of the way. Make it priority one.

Your soul came to Earth to get a physical Earth experience. If focusing on other dimensions of awareness takes you away from your Earth experience, refrain from doing that until you can maintain a grounded consciousness, which means being fully able to function in your day-to-day activities.

Some people daydream and live everywhere but in the present moment. Become increasingly aware of when your motivation for doing something is to escape your present life challenges emotionally, mentally, physically and spiritually. Self-awareness is the key to growing and grounding, for no other is responsible for you but you.

ENERGETIC ATTACHMENT TO OTHERS

Let us explore the cause of attachment to another. Many people will go into another person's energy field and *attach* to their field energetically. This has no benefit. Always stay centered in your energy field. It is important to observe another's energies without attaching to them.

Think of your energy field as a storehouse of various energies that are uniquely yours, no one else's. Just the same, other people's energies are theirs, not yours.

1. When you attach into someone you extend a cord, metaphorically, and plug into their field of energy.

2. Now you are susceptible to their energies. Their energies will imbalance your energies and contribute to illness.

There are few valid reasons for ever going into someone else's field of energy. One such occasion is during intimate moments of procreation. As a counselor, it could also be a way to guide someone in a session.

However, as a healer, counselor or parent guiding another, you will simply read the person's field rather than actually attach to it. When you read a field of energy you perceive it but do not entangle in it. Even so, when you read a field, you need to make sure you completely energetically detach from them so they do not affect you in a detrimental way. You may use the grounding exercise to do this. By using it, you will automatically ground and center your energies within you.

Immediately after going into another person's field, detach the energetic cords.

People consciously create cords from fear-related intentions or misguided teachings. As a result, it drains their energy field. They actually take on the other person's experience energetically and sometimes physically. This is not an action of the person you attach into. It is an action of you who attaches to the person. Unless the person you attach to has a similar subconscious belief system of attaching to your energy field, they will not experience what you experience. You would not affect them in any way.

When you attach to their field you are creating a bridge for their thoughts, emotions and physical energies to come into your field. To the degree you are open and choose to experience their energies is the extent you will experience them. For instance, many healers as well as confidants feel it is beneficial to help someone by taking on their illness or emotions. It Is Not. Have you heard the phrase, "I felt what they were going through"? Some people actually expect another to go through things with them. It's common to hear people say things like, "Can't you feel what I'm going through; don't you care?"

You are responsible for your energy and experiences and no one else's. Never go into someone's energy field with an intention or belief that you can take on their energies because you will. If you take on their energies, you are not present with your own experience. You thereby unground yourself resulting in your experiences not counting. It is a fine line between when you are grounded and when you are not. Embrace your life for what it is. Role model to children what it means to be present and grounded.

141

One way you can be certain that you will not attach into another person's field is by honoring their free will. When you have an agenda and an attachment to that agenda happening a certain way, you create an energetic cord. People will always disagree. Children will always disagree. You will never meet someone who will agree with you on everything and many times they will see vitally important perspectives differently from you. The key to being completely free from attachments is to honor the free will of all people. By not being attached to the way someone must perform, you no longer need to stay plugged in to their energy field. This plugging in or attaching into someone's energy is an attempt to *control* them.

The belief that one can control another is not a realistic concept. An attempt to control others is really an attempt to control your own life and it will create an energetic attachment every time you do it.

Honor the free will and unique differences that others embody without a rigid attempt to make them different and you will know true freedom.

ADVANCED GROUNDING: SPLITTING YOUR CONSCIOUSNESS

Do you tend to live in the future or the past? Is it challenging to be focused and present in the moment? If so, you are more than likely ungrounded. Practice becoming centered with the experience you are presently in.

The past is a tool to learn from. By learning from past experiences you can change the present. The future is a tool for setting goals. By projecting a possible outcome and setting goals you have something to guide you in the present.

People who live in the future and past are not as productive as those who are grounded in the present. To live in the past, future or any other dimension of creation for that matter, you are choosing to not be grounded in the present. This means you are missing valuable experiences in the moment that you would have received if you were present for them. Look around you. There is so much beauty to take in.

Teach children what the present and past are used for. Also teach them about the imaginary realm of creation. It is okay to play with the imaginary realm. However, it is imperative to be grounded in the present at all times while doing so. You can create with your imagination and at the same time be grounded in the present. In this way, the imaginary realm is not a living mechanism; rather it is an enhancement to everyday life.

Teach children how to be aware of the physical and nonphysical spaces. Show them how to be aware of what is going on outside and inside of them.

Splitting your consciousness allows you to ground your consciousness in more than one place at the same time. It is crucial to not attempt this until you are completely grounded in where your body is first. When I speak of consciousness, I mean the awareness of your personality that your soul created. It is advantageous to split your consciousness. It will take practice to do this without actually ungrounding. It has been termed *out of body travel*, *astral travel* and other such names. People have ungrounded themselves as they've attempted to split their consciousness. The idea of staying grounded when splitting your consciousness may be foreign to those who practice such experiences. The key is to be aware of what is going on in your present location and at the same time be aware of another location. The other location may be in the Nonphysical or Physical Universe. Know the imaginary realm I spoke of earlier could be a mental manifestation in the Physical Universe or a real occurrence in the Nonphysical Universe.

The Nonphysical Universe is where your soul and other souls who guide you into your destiny reside. It is your home away from home. Your true home where your soul was born from and will return to when your total soul destiny is completed is the *God Universe*, known simply as *God* or in other words the *Source Universe*. This universe is the Source of your existence. It is the universe from which I am speaking to you. The *Physical Universe* is where your personality resides that your soul has created to receive its physical experience. Your soul is connected to your physical personality, however your soul primarily resides in the *Nonphysical Universe*, due to the vibrational difference between the Physical and Nonphysical Universes. Your personality is the liaison, if you will, between your nonphysical soul experience and the Physical Universe where your personality presently resides.

There are infinite points of grounded consciousness. These infinite points make up the matrix of creation. Imagine a web with infinite points on the matrix. At any time you may ground your consciousness to one of the other points and experience it. The objective when splitting your consciousness is to be clear and accurate in where you go and what you do.

Splitting your consciousness with a grounded awareness is advanced for humanity at this time. There was a time when it was more common.

Splitting your consciousness is different than ungrounding. When you split your consciousness you stay grounded where your physical body is; also, you ground to where your physical body is not, this is where your consciousness splits to.

Your soul is an observer for the most part. Your soul can at times engage in your personality's experience if it is necessary to help your personality gain a specific insight. This would be called *intuition* or *impingement*. When you are impinged upon by your soul, you receive it as a hunch or a more apparent influence such as a voice in your head or a strong vision. Regardless of how your soul communicates a message, your personality must be grounded to receive the message accurately. In order to receive accurate, clear intuitive information from your *spiritual guides* (souls that assist you nonphysically), God, as well as other human beings, you must be grounded.

There are two aspects to rejuvenation while asleep: one, for your personality and two, for your soul.

When you go to sleep your soul leaves your body and your personality's consciousness goes into a rejuvenating experience of dreams and healing.

1. The *body* goes into deep sleep or hibernation. Then, the personality may tend to its needs such as changing beliefs and processing emotions.

2. The *soul* leaves the body and crosses over completely to the Nonphysical Universe where it too rejuvenates.

When your soul is dwelling in the Nonphysical Universe during sleep, it engages in other activities including teaching, guiding, counseling or any number of other pertinent tasks contributing to its greater destiny. Sometimes your soul hangs out with friends, as you would call them, and checks in on your soul mates. Every night while your body sleeps your soul leaves the body. This is the only consistent time your soul leaves its body. Other than a few exceptions your soul is always grounded in your physical body. The soul may leave its body and unground from the physical experience during near-death experiences or traumatic events such as a coma. The personality has no control over the soul leaving or staying. It is the choice of the soul.

The soul will attempt to impress upon the personality to stay and work through the imbalances that are causing it to leave the physical body experience. In this world there are many examples of why people unground. Anything that takes you out of the present will affect your ability to ground.

If you choose to split your consciousness and simultaneously ground it in another part of creation, you are not violating universal laws. Rather you are using a powerful tool that will benefit you and your children. Everyone splits their consciousness; it is called multitasking, daydreaming, etc. But most people unground to do these things.

Remember, being grounded allows you to relate and communicate with others in the grounded Earth space. The goal is to practice being grounded where you are and bi-locating your consciousness somewhere else. This may lead to you being able to transport your physical body somewhere else or create a second body to participate in another location. When you split and ground your consciousness in two or more locations, you are *bi-locating*. The degree you can focus and master this will determine your accuracy and impact in any location. There are many places to split your consciousness to other than a physical Earth location.

Do you notice how a child's attention can wander? Their attention wanders because they split their consciousness to other places in creation and lose their grounding. This is common with ADD and ADHD among other categorized imbalances. What really happens, for the most part, is children create a habit of splitting their consciousness by ungrounding. This leaves them unfocused, dazed and confused.

The chilling epidemic is how children are learning to be ungrounded and choose this space because it is where they can relate to other kids who are also ungrounded.

Children are brilliant. Their brilliance goes unmanifested however, when they are ungrounded. If you can get today's children to ground, they will manifest their brilliance and astonish everyone.

CHILD GROUNDING EXERCISE

1. **Make sure you are grounded.**

2. **Start by holding the child's hand.**

3. **Ask them to take three deep breaths from their belly.** The sign of a grounded person is when they breathe from their belly; you will see their belly go in and out. An ungrounded person will breathe from the mid to top of their chest.

4. **Slowly have them bring their eyes to their feet and think themselves into their feet until their feet *feel* heavy.**

5. **Have the child take slow, deep breaths until their racing mind slows and they are grounded.** Explain to

them that the mind is not meant to race as it normally does for them.

6. **Have the child ask God or their body to ground them.** Have them tell God or their body that they want to be fully present for their experience.

Even if the child doesn't comprehend what is being said, you will intuitively send the message to them and their subconscious will respond. This is also true for infants and babies.

Once the child is grounded, practice with them how to split their consciousness. It can be a lot of fun if you get creative with them. This will also help you bring out your inner child.

Ask the child if they can remember when they daydream. Many children split their consciousness by daydreaming before they go to sleep, such as when you read them a bedtime story their consciousness splits and goes into a fantasy of the story. Maybe they pretend they are in the story. When they share an experience with you, explain to them how to stay present here and now, and be there at the same time. The idea is they do not have to leave here to go there. By staying present here and grounding there as well, it will be a fuller and more memorable experience for them. Simply let them know that they can be in two places at once.

EXERCISES ON SPLITTING YOUR CONSCIOUSNESS

This can be a lot of fun. You can do these exercises over the phone or in person. You are not limited by distance when playing with exercises in splitting your consciousness. Practice makes perfect.

SPLITTING CONSCIOUSNESS FLASH CARD EXERCISE

1. Draw some shapes, numbers, letters or other symbols on blank flash cards, one symbol per card.

2. Place one card at a time behind something so the child can't see the card.

3. Ask the child to split their consciousness to where the flash card is so they may see the symbol on it.

SPLITTING CONSCIOUSNESS OBJECT EXERCISE

1. Use a variety of colored marbles, dice, stones or other objects.

2. Hold one object in your closed hand so the child can't see the object. You could also have them close their eyes and place it in their closed hand.

3. Ask the child to split their consciousness to where the object is to see what color it is.

These types of exercises will teach you and children how to be totally grounded. If you can be grounded in two places at one time, you can definitely be grounded in one place. Take time to give this gift to yourself and share it with the world.

Ask children where they split their consciousness to and *listen* to what they say.

- This will give you a window into their world and experiences.

- They will feel like you relate with and understand them better.

- Your relationship with them will grow.

- The separation that you and the child felt will start to disappear.

As a result, they will perform better and develop properly.

Children are functioning with greater awareness and possibilities than most adults. They are not more capable human beings than adults, but they have not yet shut down their soul-based nature. Therefore, they are more receptive.

With practice you may expand your awareness to easily perceive the other parts of creation. Every time your personality accepts a belief that supports the *ego-based perspective*, you muffle or close down your awareness to perceive these other dimensions of reality. Every time your personality accepts and operates from the *soul-based perspective*, your awareness opens, becomes clearer and more capable. Learn children's clear soul-based perspective and live it. For the kids who have already accepted many ego-based beliefs, you will be on a journey with them to clear and return to innocence.

Consciousness is simply your personality's awareness. It would benefit you to split your consciousness, to some degree, between where your nonphysical guides reside in the Nonphysical Universe and your physical life in the Physical Universe. That way you can be open to their wisdom, guidance and healing in any moment. Be sure you stay grounded, as most people unground to contact nonphysical guides.

Make sure if you split your consciousness that you are first able to remain grounded in one location.

You have advanced in your ability to ground your consciousness when you can truly accept all of your emotions, thoughts, actions and physicality, as well as your past and potential future experiences which include your relationships with other people. Then, you have accomplished step one of The Five Accomplishments.

At this point, you are permanently grounded, except by unseen physical circumstances that would cause your consciousness to unground. For example, this could take the form of chemicals taken into your body, radiation poisoning, illness or severe physical trauma. In any case, you would be physically forced to unground via an outside force rather than by your conscious or subconscious beliefs. Accidents of this nature are rare. The most common case of this is when parents do drugs or smoke and kids unground as a result of the toxins inhaled from the smoke. Please note that the smoke from drugs or tobacco will stay on clothes and any other material for as long as months, affecting the wellbeing of a child or adult.

Accomplishment One: Be present with and accept every part of your physical experience.

The journey to being grounded in everything you experience is a cycle of sorts.

1. You will go through accomplishments one to four enough times so you can truly *accept* every experience of your life.

2. Until the point of unconditional acceptance, you may bounce to accomplishment one from two, three or four and move forward in the process from there.

3. After you ground, move on to accomplishment two where you will *get real with your life* one situation at a time.

If a situation arises that causes you to unground because you do not want to face it, you must go back to accomplishment one to ground before revisiting the situation. Ungrounding in this way is usually subconscious and sometimes the person is unaware that they unground, especially if it is a pattern for them to do so. In essence, you are facing the reality of your life—past, present and future.

The same goes for accomplishment three and four. As you delve deeper into an experience of your life and reach closer to the experience of your soul, you may have situations arise that you do not accept. If this is the case and you unground, you will go back to step one and work from there. It is necessary to be grounded with each accomplishment. When you unconditionally accept your life in its entirety, you have accomplished step five: *Initiation of the Soul*.

Remember, you don't have to agree with something to accept it. Rather just embrace the fact it is happening and that it is okay it is happening, even if you disagree with it. If you cannot accept everything, first get grounded and then move to step two to *get real* with the experiences you are not accepting.

Next let's explore ways for you to get real with your experiences once you do get grounded.

Chapter 14

ACCOMPLISHMENT TWO: GET REAL WITH YOUR LIFE

I t is essential for children to be completely *real* or *authentic* with their life. They tend to learn from adults how to escape life and this adds to their challenge of remaining grounded. The reason someone would not get real with their life or outer world is because it is too traumatic for them or it would be upsetting if they got real with it. In relationships the imbalanced ways spouses treat each other and the violation of universal laws adds to the struggle of getting real with life. The past regret of situations that one blocks in order to go on with their day-to-day life also makes it challenging to get real with one's life. In some cases the lack of getting real is a living mechanism, because if one was to actually look at the experience and accept what happened, they would have a nervous breakdown, become suicidal or experience any number of other conditions.

There is no reason to bring something up if the person is not ready for it. However, I will show you how to be ready for it.

Listen to your *self-talk* while you are getting real with your life. It will tell you exactly what you need to get real with. Speak it out loud and record yourself if you must. This also works with children. Listen to what they say and believe what they say. Then, attempt to comprehend and balance their discomfort. If what they share is not imbalanced there is nothing to balance, just simply listen.

Truly attempt to see through children's eyes and perceive from their vantage point. It may be the one thing that creates trust and understanding between you and your child. In the end it will be the only thing that gives the child an understanding of you. You will share your perspectives, not overshadowing the child's, and through the sharing of perspectives the child learns and becomes a capable human being. This is advantageous for both you and the child.

1. You learn how to observe and listen.

2. Then, share from the soul-based perspective.

3. As a result, the child feels heard and understood which creates confidence in the child and gives them an experience of soul-based living.

Thank you for being patient with your children and creating a world that feels safe for them to exist in . . . a world where they can be heard and grounded, accepting their feelings and thoughts about life.

Infants are a whole other reality when you attempt to share with them the realness of their life. Infants communicate through intuition mostly so practice intuitive communication with them. When you communicate with infants, physically or nonphysically, be incredibly focused and clear on what you are intending to express.

Please make sure that your inner experience translates into your outer expression clearly. For instance, if you get angry inside, possibly from an inconvenience an infant creates for you, allow yourself to express the emotion with the infant in as soul-based a way as possible. Consequently, they will learn how to clearly communicate instead of unclearly. Then, they will absolutely be real with their world and not learn to cover up their feelings and thoughts with inconsistent outer expression through action and words. It is more important to be *honest* with your newborn child instead of inauthentic.

You have learned you should be a certain way with an infant such as smiling and laughing with silly expressions. Do this only if you truly feel like doing it.

Whatever you feel and think, please be *transparent* with children so they know you are being real with them. Thus, they learn to be real and express themselves clearly which frees them from the difficulty of hiding things, even from themselves.

Chapter 15

ACCOMPLISHMENT THREE: GET REAL WITH YOUR INNER WORLD

T he last step before merging with your soul is to *get real with God*. In order to get real with God you must get real with yourself, which includes your innermost experiences. We can call this your *inner world*. To the degree you get real, embrace and accept your innermost experiences of life, reciprocates a similar acceptance and unity with God.

Getting real with your inner world is by far the most challenging accomplishment. It may take years or even your entire lifetime to work through. It's really up to you. The *contraction* of one's authentic feelings and thoughts is a result of the conditional ego-based perspective that was accepted at some point from humanity. This contraction gives the perception of one's soul being dimmed because one's authentic feelings and thoughts are more challenging to face and express.

For that reason, you are on a *treasure hunt*, literally in most cases. It is as if you buried a treasure and then covered all signs of the burial.

For most their entire life, to some degree, has been one in-authentic experience after another. Many mystics have called this the *illusion*. You created beliefs that cover the *truth* of who you are and the Universe, only to replace the truth with cryptic riddles and complicated philosophies that take you away and hold you away from your truth, the real power that lies within you right now. You have done this because your parents and teachers learned it from their role models. It was then passed down to you. This burying of the authentic self has happened for countless generations.

The *treasure* is the *root experience* where you accepted the belief that is creating your present experience. Take a look at your entire life and attempt to locate the roots of your present experiences. As you do, you will often find the root experiences originate when you were a child with one or both of your primary caretakers.

The treasure is your destination. We will search and find it every time. I will make sure you are helped in the process; just call on God.

There are examples of beliefs listed previously in this book. You may reference them and expand upon them with your own examples.

Beliefs that trigger reactionary instinctual responses give you the feeling of being *powerless* to change your life experience.

Beliefs that allow you to choose your responses give you a feeling of being *powerful* to change your life experience.

The following examples illustrate instinctual and chosen responses to life situations to help you understand your beliefs and the root experiences where they were accepted.

EXAMPLES OF INSTINCTUAL RESPONSES

1. *BELIEF: I fear what others think about me.*

   ROOT: My mother and father fear what others think about them. I accepted the belief from them when I was very young. I was not accepted by kids throughout school and that reinforced the belief. It started when I was seven. I feel like others are criticizing me even if they are not and it bothers me.

2. *BELIEF: I procrastinate.*

   ROOT: My father procrastinates on many things. I accepted this belief from him when I was three. When my parents asked me to do something, I would procrastinate. Now it affects my career.

3. *BELIEF: I'm not good enough.*

ROOT: My mother and father feel they are not good enough. I accepted this when I was five. In school I did not feel good enough about myself to make friends. Now I'm shy in social settings and it's difficult to start conversations with people I don't know.

4. *BELIEF: I am sensitive to other people's thoughts, emotions and physical energies.*

ROOT: I accepted this belief of intuitively feeling into another's energy field from my mother and father. As a result, it ungrounds me. I did this to better understand my parent's intentions so I could feel safer and more acceptable when I was three. Now it debilitates me, making me tired and emotional. Once I picked up the pain of someone's headache.

5. *BELIEF: Eating sugar fulfills me.*

ROOT: My family and friends indulge in sugar. I accepted the belief from them when I was two that sugar is good and desirable. It's really hard to not eat sugar. I feel I have no control.

6. *BELIEF: My bladder releases urine at inopportune times.*

ROOT: I learned from the world, collectively, at the youngest age that when you reach sixty, you lose control of your bladder. I feel helpless because I can't control my bladder.

EXAMPLES OF CHOSEN RESPONSES

1. *BELIEF: I am patient.*

ROOT: I created a new belief when I was twenty-eight that I am patient and observe situations while asserting my truth in a nonjudgmental way. I learned this from my spiritual mentor. This belief has given me more peace and health.

2. *BELIEF: My soul's destiny is my priority.*

ROOT: I created a new belief when I was thirty that my soul's destiny is more important than anything else. I learned this from my spiritual support system. Now I live each day feeling I have purpose and direction.

3. *BELIEF: I don't yell at or physically hit my children.*

ROOT: My mother and father did not yell at or physically hit me. I learned this from them when I was very little and I continue to choose this belief for myself. There is more harmony in my family as a result of this belief.

4. *BELIEF: I accept others unconditionally.*

163

ROOT: I created a new belief when I was in my forties to unconditionally love and accept everyone. I accepted this belief from a book I read.

5. *BELIEF: Eating healthy food helps me feel more energy.*

ROOT: My mother eats extremely healthy. I accepted this belief from her when I was two. I feel more energy and I feel better when I eat healthy food, so I continue to choose this belief about food.

6. *BELIEF: I levitate objects and it is easy.*

ROOT: I created a new belief when I was sixty-five that I can levitate objects with my intention anytime I want to. I accepted this belief from watching a movie.

MAPPING YOUR INNER WORLD EXERCISE

The exercise below creates a *treasure map* so you may understand yourself better. Then, you have the power to recreate the beliefs within your mind that trigger instinctual responses to beliefs that produce chosen responses.

1. Make a two-column list of your beliefs by completely getting real with all parts of your life. One column is for the beliefs that produce *chosen responses* and the other column is for beliefs that produce *instinctual responses*.

2. Below each belief explain the *root experience* where you accepted the belief, to the best of your memory.

By creating these two lists, you will begin to know your personality, its limitations and unbounded freedom. In order to help anyone, including children, first understand and help yourself. As primary caretakers your children more than likely learned most of their core beliefs from you. By understanding your core beliefs, you will understand how to help your children.

GETTING REAL WITH YOUR INNER WORLD EXERCISE

The following exercise will help you to get real with your inner world so you can list your instinctual and chosen responses, root beliefs and where you accepted them.

1. **Take deep breaths.**

   You are the center of creation. Creation happens around you and how you perceive it is a result of your beliefs.

2. **Take responsibility for your beliefs that have attracted the people, places and things connected to your current situation.**

   As you become clear within yourself, you will remember your feelings and thoughts about yourself, everyone and everything. This is beneficial, even if the feelings are hard for you to feel.

3. **Continue to breathe deeply.**

4. **Remember your relationship with your parents.** Remember how it felt to be held in their arms. If they didn't ever hold you, feel what that felt like.

5. **Remember your past experiences and live them out fully.** Replay them so you can be totally real with them.

   Follow the experiences down deeper to other feelings and thoughts. You will find how different time periods and seemingly unconnected experiences begin to show you patterns. These patterns begin to reveal your beliefs creating them.

   Eventually you will be taken to the feelings you had as a child. Your recognition of these feelings helps you to understand your present life experiences.

   Nothing is ever lost. Your memory is astounding. It takes a brave person to remember who they are and how they really feel towards their mother, father and siblings. It requires patience and love to accept the things that you remember. You are worth it.

6. **Now express yourself to me, exactly how you feel.** Take as long as you need. Don't hold back. Express what is present on your heart and mind, as if I'm with you physically. Open up to me and share. I am here with you now.

7. **Good. Now express to me exactly how you feel about the feelings you just expressed.** How did it feel to be

so vulnerable and share from the depths of your heart and soul?

Remember you are not those feelings, but those feelings came from you somewhere. It is okay to be present with their source.

8. **Now let yourself feel where the feelings came from.** What experience comes to your mind? When did you first notice feeling this way? Why? Who, directly or indirectly, exemplified the beliefs and taught you to feel this way?

MAPPING YOUR EXPERIENCES EXERCISE

Create several two-column lists of beliefs that produce chosen and instinctual responses, as you did in the Mapping Your Inner World Exercise. Again, explain beneath each belief the root experience where you accepted it. These lists will focus on specific experiences you have.

Create this two-column list for:

1. How you experience your child.

2. How you experience the rest of the world including people, places and things.

3. How you experience yourself.

MAPPING A CHILD'S EXPERIENCES EXERCISE

Examine your relationship with your child. Step into their shoes and even include them in this exercise by asking them questions, to better understand them. Now create several two-column lists of beliefs that produce chosen and instinctual responses for them. Once again, explain beneath each belief the root experience where they accepted it. These lists will focus on specific experiences that your child has.

Create this two-column list for:

1. How your child experiences you.

2. How they experience the rest of the world including people, places, and things.

3. How they experience themselves.

These lists should be very congruent. If they are not congruent, there is an inconsistency within one's interpretation and expression of their life. Look at this. The inconsistency would be emphasized by one's inability to express their inner world to the outer world through spoken word, writing or other ways of communicating, but especially energy.

Children's subconscious beliefs manifest physically into the world, even if the child is unaware of them or doesn't clearly communicate them.

1. *Reveal* their subconscious beliefs.

2. *Comprehend* them.

3. Help the child *decide* what they would like to do with them.

Basically you will help the child discern if their beliefs are helping them or if they want to change them.

The child's age will determine how much input you have as an authority figure. Ultimately it is up to the child to voice what beliefs they want to change. Even if you intuitively communicate with their subconscious mind or soul to find out what they want for themselves, their personality must be a part of their programming or reprogramming. It is their life on Earth and they are required under universal laws to be included in the programming of their minds.

When exploring the child's beliefs take note of inconsistencies between different parts of the child's life. Ideally they will see all aspects of their life from the same viewpoint. If there are inconsistencies, you need to explore why they exist and help shift them.

If there are more instinctual responses than chosen responses, you may make one list longer than the other or vice versa. It begins to look more and more like a map. You are putting together maps of subconscious beliefs to better see the big picture of who you and your children are. By seeing the big picture, how all the pieces fit together, you can better change the instinctual responses to chosen ones. This way you will be more and more enabled to depend on your choices to guide you through your life, rather than your reactions, unless of course it is your chosen response to react. This can seem a bit complicated initially, but you will comprehend it more as you play with it.

Find the root experiences where you accepted the beliefs creating instinctual responses and change them to chosen ones. By changing your beliefs, you will be in greater command of your life experience. As a result, your soul becomes the driver and your life is forever changed. Let us truly celebrate your accomplishments as you learn to choose every experience you have. This is when life becomes more amazing, joyful and fun!

In order to accomplish what you have set out to do, to respond in an observing and chosen manner rather than a seemingly instinctual manner, you will absolutely need to trust yourself more than you ever have. I'm talking about unequivocal trust in every word, action and thought you have. *Believe* in yourself enough to *trust* yourself. This will create motivation that anything is possible, even bending your perspective of space and time. When you notice just how flexible creation is, you will have a means to practice and create anything you desire as it accords with your soul's destiny on Earth at this time.

We congratulate you as you push through the brittle walls that have kept you from really owning your authentic power as a human being. Believe you will amaze yourself, friends and all, and you will. Believe you will be an example of change and growth for your children to follow, and it will happen. It already is. Celebrate the attention you have given yourself for personal growth and heart-centered love. Be well to your mind. Learn to really love your mind by becoming exactly what you choose to become. As you do, by your example, so does the world.

Now that you have truly empowered yourself and support reflection within, you are ready to shift your beliefs and create the life of your dreams.

I will be bold and honest with you. You may indeed change your life completely overnight. You may also take time. It is truly up to you. It depends on your *openness* and *willingness* to be changed. Changing your life is a step into the unknown. It requires trust and faith in yourself and God.

You are safe and you will be provided for.

AFFIRMATION OF CHANGE

Now Say:

"I Am Ready To Change My Life.

I give it to you God and I am aware that I will never be the same person.

There are reasons why I am becoming different and I leave those in your hands God.

I am growing in many ways because I am fulfilling my soul's purpose on Earth and I love myself unconditionally. Thus, I am an example to the world.

The world will experience peace and liberty for all people. I rejoice now knowing that this world is already here. We must see it, as the bird high above can see the beautiful landscapes; it is all one scene and it is all majesty.

I am here succeeding in my soul's purpose on Earth.

Thank you God for your patience with me and support unconditionally."

Blessings to you my child . . .

Now that you've given your life over to me, I will change your life with little effort.

DISCOVERING PHYSICALITY

Remember when you were very little, just barely able to walk. Your attention would go to everything it could. You were extremely cunning in your search for answers to this inevitable physical existence. You knew on some level you were stuck in it, and while here, you would do your best with the provided circumstances.

You found, even at this young age, there were obstacles which included:

- The fire on the stove was too hot to directly touch.

- If you urinated in your pants it was wet and uncomfortable.

- How your caretakers responded to you determined how you received love.

- Walking creates many more options than crawling.

As you acquainted yourself with these perspectives and many others, your ability to evolve and reside in the physical world, Earth, was progressing.

You could adapt to situations as they presented themselves, adaptations such as:

- Being patient with those around you.

- Loving for the sake of loving.

- Giving for the sake of giving.

- Survival of physical living.

- Intuitively knowing or feeling if a person or situation was beneficial for you or not.

- Learning what is customary with individuals, groups and cultures of people.

You actually built your entire perspective of physical living based on your obstacles and freedoms from infancy to adolescence and into adulthood. There are countless reasons why you would limit yourself with obstacles and block yourself with inabilities to live a balanced physical life, but there is only one reason to live free and in accordance with universal laws. That reason is because you are a *free* soul that lives in accordance with universal laws. Why would it be any different when you come down to Earth as a soul to physically live? In the broader agreement and understanding of existence by all souls and God, universal laws are followed willingly for the benefit of Creation. However, on this unique plane of existence called the Physical Universe, you can forget, miss and ultimately negate the very nature of who you are. It's time to wake up and know the reality of what you are, and live it, now. You are capable of realizing this *one reason* to change and letting go of every other motivation to not change. You are brave. You will look back on this life, the life you chose to stand like a soul and live like a soul.

BEING ON PATH

There are countless examples of people who attempt to misdirect themselves by inadvertently causing blocks and obstacles to happen in their life.

Imagine yourself on a long straight road. By using this image, you will accomplish more in a shorter amount of time. This visualization is used by mystics to create balance in their focus and direction of life. It will keep you, at least subconsciously, moving ahead and continuing in a forward direction.

Many have talked about taking two steps forward and one step back. In this case, you would not have a straight path but a windy one. This is not needed. You may have a straight and forward journey where you take no steps backward. It has been a collective belief that life must be hard and difficult with winding roads. It may be like that, but it doesn't have to be.

Life will always present challenge, for the reason of living is to grow through the challenge of making choices. However, you may have the challenge of choice and at the same time be taking each step forward and never reverse or leave your path. It is possible and will be exceptionally common in the coming years as more people choose to live from their soul. Soul-based living is here and will continue to manifest. As you change enough of your beliefs and live in a way that moves you in a straight and forward direction on your soul's path, you will be an example for all to see this.

SHARING

Tell your friends about your challenges. The more you share about your choices with others, the more options will be revealed to you. This is to be done in a natural, nonchalant way, not a forced or obsessive way. Let others know how you are, even if they do not ask you. If they don't want to hear it, they can find another friend or choose not to be in your life.

➤ Do you really want people in your life that are not interested in you?

If you have disinterested people in your life, change the belief that is bringing them in and bring new people into your life that will support you by listening and sharing perspectives with you. If you accomplish this, you will significantly change your destiny, and each step you take will be forward because you're free from fearing the challenges and choices that follow.

Peace is something that comes from within. It is created by your willingness to accept yourself. One way of practicing inner peace is to share your experiences with people in your life, even strangers, especially strangers. If you can feel comfortable sharing your life with strangers, you have accomplished self-mastery in a major way. When I say share, I mean share your innermost feelings and thoughts no matter how you think the stranger may react to them. Be you, not based on anything outside of you.

Thank you for considering this. It will ultimately be your choice to stand strong in who you are and share fearlessly.

SELF-PLEASURE

Self-pleasure is monumental in the evolution of this world's consciousness. The nature of *self-pleasure* means *self-love*. Self-pleasure has been construed as *evil* or *negative* in the past by being woven into religions and tagged with the stigma that God will punish you, and your soul is in jeopardy if you pleasure yourself. Consequently, there are strong generational beliefs that steer you away from natural, nurturing self-pleasures.

Loving self-pleasures include:

- Relating to your body in a loving, nurturing way by massage, caressing and accepting its nakedness.

- Treating yourself to foods your body truly desires.

- Giving your body, mind and spirit rest from the physical life.

- Unconditionally receiving love from others.

- Believing in your power to arouse spiritual and psychic energies for healing and comfort.

- Knowing you're not alone and experiencing the pleasure of communing with your nonphysical friends.

- Surrounding yourself with people that respect and accommodate your love for yourself.

These are but a few natural, nonsexual ways of pleasuring yourself. Teach children it is okay to pleasure themselves and to practice it. You could have a special time set aside for pleasuring yourself as a family or group.

It matters not what others may think of a group pleasuring themselves. The collective consciousness is strong regarding pleasuring the self. There will be resistance to this new concept. However, it is one of the most significant break-throughs you can make with yourself and others.

The teaching of pleasuring the self is mainly rooted in the universal *law of self-love* and laws under it. Experiment and enjoy who you are. Eventually you will find self-pleasure in everything you do and this is called self-love, meaning that everything you do is a result of your love for yourself. By putting self-love first in your life, you are pleasured in every moment of your life. Lives can be totally changed with this one concept alone. It will open doors to other beautiful vistas that this world has deemed as unholy.

When you are truly free to love yourself and accept the world unconditionally, you will be living enlightened from the perspective of your soul.

Chapter 16

NEW PARADIGM OF EDUCATION

C hildren are faced with an insidious experience at school. It is important to train kids to be as resilient as possible when the peer pressure of classmates is pushing them in a direction that violates their truth. The child needs to be included in the choice to do or not do something. But ultimately you are the caretaker and you are responsible for molding their choices and setting *stern* but *loving* guidelines. As a result, they may understand their relationship with others who are pressuring them to be a certain way.

Kids will be kids in some ways. There is a degree of childishness kids will explore.

Within this there will be guidance that you need to assert so the child may grow into a mature human being.

What determines being mature? Becoming *mature* is following universal laws and naturally developing into an adult. Teach universal laws to your children by being an example of them. It is that simple. Your job is to follow universal laws and exemplify them to children.

When children ask you questions, explain the reasoning behind your answers to them. Treat every second you have with your child as a participatory experience in their evolution. Seize the opportunity and never deny a child their right to evolve into a clear perspective of living. Always put their wellbeing as a priority and live in accordance with universal laws.

It is always beneficial to renounce any thoughts of changing the child for the sake of your own comfort. This is something that has plagued this world for millennia, sorry to say. I am giving you a means of delivering your world from the years of bondage and slavery. What is a slave? A slave is someone who is under the control of another. The caretaker-child relationship has been slavery for the most part. Caretakers disrespect the child's soul through controlling the child. How do you change this? Decide you will become a *guide* for the child instead of a *dictator*.

> ➤ How many times did your parents dictate what you should do and how to do it?

I believe within your heart is the ability to *unconditionally love* your children. Whether you choose to do it is up to you.

Realize the enormity of the affect you will have on your soul's greater destiny by empowering children today. You have one life to live so *live* it. When you physically die and your soul chooses to come down to Earth again, forgetting everything from this life, you start new, fresh. While you are here this time, use your awakened personality to seize the opportunity to love children more. As a result, next time you incarnate, you will have parents, teachers and leaders who are more loving because they are the children of today. You have been through so many experiences in this life. Use your experiences to motivate you into loyalty to your soul and its purpose. Then, use your newfound strength to turn the tide of this corrupt civilization to one that honors the soul in all and surrenders to God unconditionally. Beginnings start with endings.

Your absence from children's lives creates a feeling of abandonment causing a misunderstanding of love. Abandonment is a common experience for people. Children feel increasingly alone without anyone who can understand and comfort them. People feel alone because their caretakers energetically abandoned them when they were children. This was due to their caretaker's own imbalances.

If a caretaker feels overwhelmed, the child is the victim.

If a caretaker feels depressed, the child is the victim.

When a caretaker is imbalanced in any way, their attention is taken away from the child in beneficial ways and is redirected back at the child in unbeneficial ways. Most caretakers are unaware of this pattern.

Show children that you want to understand them. Really learn to listen on all levels of interaction with them. Listen to what is obvious or clear and what may be hidden or unclear expressions from children. Be aware of what is seen and unseen, heard and unheard, felt and unfelt, known and unknown. Your duty is to learn to *listen* in ways you previously haven't.

Be *patient* and aware of children. Don't always be the *impatient* rule setter. You don't want to lose your respect as an elder; however you also don't want to lose respect for your child as a pure vessel of untapped innocence. Let the child be the role model at times. Children are born with invaluable wisdom on how to live a balanced life. Your key contributions to a child's viewpoint of life are insights for navigating through humanity's many rules and customs in today's world.

When children are old enough to ask questions, they are old enough to receive answers.

Children ask questions for reasons. It's vital to their growth to receive answers. The common belief of caretakers that kids are not old enough to know certain things is a misconception. There is no age that children should be prohibited from information. Any information can be shared in a way that is relative to where a child is at in their evolution. Listen to what the child is really asking and tailor the answer to their request. Being receptive to children's questions and thoughtfully answering them will inspire them to develop and mature far faster than neglecting them. Please embrace this reasoning.

Therefore, if a child asks you why you did something please respond. You have a right under the law of free will to not respond, however it benefits both of you to respond. It benefits you because honesty and sharing are part of balanced living. The child benefits from you sharing experiences. They learn how to better be a human being.

Please do not fear that by sharing imbalances about yourself or the world with kids that they will follow in those footsteps. You are their guide by the fact that you have chosen to be in their life at this time. Learn to be transparent with them. Have no walls or judgments when sharing with children and your relationship with them will grow. You are amazing for considering such challenging concepts to follow. I bless you.

Let us discover new ways of teaching today's children. It takes great determination to change the education systems of this world but it is deeply needed. I will start with an overall concept of why we would change education in the first place. We need to look at your commitment to your children, the education systems in place and how transitioning into a new way of educating people can benefit the world.

COMPETITION CONSCIOUSNESS

The key to human dignity is pride. Pride is by no means unbalanced unless it is taken out of context with fear. *Pride* is self-love of one's accomplishments without placing a judgment in comparison to others. When pride is taken out of context using fear-driven motives, it can be destructive for everyone involved.

Unfortunately pride has been unbalanced in relation to educating children. Humanity has fixated on intellectual superiority, basing its education systems on this fanaticism. Furthermore, this ego-based competitive consciousness has induced a rift in group allegiance and support for one another. This results in children feeling like the education experience is, figuratively speaking, a *war*.

Alternative points of view on competition related to education are rare and incomplete. The few perspectives that are different have only a slice of the picture needed to create a harmonious education experience. As a result of children spending most of their earlier years in school and in situations related to school, there is a huge problem to contend with.

1. Decree to yourself and the world, both energetically and physically, that there is a problem with the paradigm of education and a great change is needed in education systems worldwide.

2. Make a commitment to yourself to participate on some level in changing how children are educated, both in schools and in your homes.

3. Identify your resources to make this change and take action.

Let us examine the current systems that educate your youth. Be honest with yourself each step of the way. When you shake your head in surprise and ask the question, "Is this really possible?" Take a deep breath and say to yourself, "Yes this is happening and I am in the middle of it."

The most vital component of education that deserves attention is how children learn. Children currently are taught to learn by cramming information into their minds. For the most part they utilize little to none of their other sensory perceptions such as their intuitive inner seeing, hearing, feeling and knowing qualities. If you deprive a child of their intuitive abilities, you will create a harder road for them.

From the very beginning, teach children about their natural intuitive four qualities of perceiving life. By doing this, you can't imagine what doors will open and milestones will be made in *one generation.* You will optimize every moment in a child's education and life. You will accomplish the greatest change needed in education. Children will integrate intuition with reasoning. Teachers and parents will be astonished when children surpass adults intellectually. They will accomplish more in two years than the current system has them accomplishing in ten. Try it and see for yourself.

Another critical change required is with the liability you place on kids if they do not pass or perform how you want. Parents, teachers and all caretakers have placed an unnecessary burden on children by creating a *reward and punishment system*. This system does not accomplish its intended purpose of allowing the child to take responsibility for their actions. It pressures kids to perform like other kids and live up to adults' expectations based on an education system that doesn't work.

You are literally setting some kids up to feel like failures and others to feel like pompous, intellectually superior, society-built heroes. You need to change this right now. It is the basis of your education consciousness on Earth. It hurts kids in many ways, both emotionally and mentally, in how they feel and think about themselves. It further manifests in many cases physically, which ages children much quicker than they would otherwise. Yes, this is truth. You may take it for what you feel is truth for you. The fact is that you base your reward and punishment systems on performance and that is not fair. Each child is unique and you are not addressing this. You are shaping kids to be like each other through performance-based reward and punishment systems.

Balanced, harmonious competition is beneficial and abides by all universal laws. Competition on this world is created with attachments to expectations that damage children's

ability to love themselves. This further dista?
from their *true calling*, which may be nothing
society is pushing on them.

Caretakers need to recognize that their kids did not come
down to Earth to be clones of them. They came down to
live, learn and possibly perform differently. Kids must not
be pressured to perform a certain way by using punish-
ments and rewards.

Rewards are to be offered to everyone *equally* across-the-
board, as a team. Therefore, if one child isn't getting it others can assist. This is the essence of rhythmic soul-based
living, group support and allegiance to one another. Once
you change the ego-based competition consciousness with
soul-based support, your world will transform in one generation.

It isn't enough that your world supports some kids and
leaves others unsupported based on the circumstances of
their upbringing. Your world purposely judges that some
kids do not deserve the same opportunity as others.

All the money spent on defense is being wasted. If the
money was directed toward helping the world through creating equality of basic needs, the world would change in
one generation.

1. Make your neighbor as important to you as your child.

2. Make your neighbor's child as important as your own.

187

3. Make the children of your enemy just as important as your own life.

4. Finally, when you seek and truly find love, you will make your enemy as important as yourself and your children. You will be unconditionally sharing with the world's people from your soul to their souls.

When everyone accomplishes this, there will no longer be war, and you will for the first time in many years know world peace. It is here.

Believe this world can change. It is called *hope*. Hold hope in your heart. If you hold hope in your heart anything may happen. I truly encourage you to remain hopeful, even through the challenging views I'm sharing with you in this book. There will be more books to follow and this world will change one way or another. It is humanity's destiny.

REVOLUTIONISM

Show children how to grow up with a gentle lean towards revolutionism. It is essential. Many individuals including governments discourage this type of language. I, for one, see no other way. It is, in essence, the very nature of a soul to rearrange and reorganize as per the situation or experience requires. It is the nature of a soul to be revolutionary to some degree. It's had an unfavorable connotation regarding the overthrowing of governments. I'm not speaking about overthrowing anything. I'm speaking about revolutionizing the way humanity exists in every way. Teaching children to have this mindset will instill in them the safety of change.

Today's children are taught that to tout or suggest change to superiors, including government, parents, teachers and adults really of any kind, results in them either being punished or inflicted with severe backlash by authority figures attempting to keep things status quo. In many respects this world is on a collision course with itself. The momentum for change that has been building within the collective consciousness is calling for a revolutionary way to better experience life.

I and all of the spirits guiding this world are committed to this revolution during this most trying time. Our hope is that we can influence enough people without breaking too many universal laws, thereby creating a complete change in the thinking and consciousness of this world's people.

Ascertain in what part you would like to participate within this revolution. I repeat, you are part of a revolution. This revolution has been talked about for ages. Did you think that it was going to be a war as some have thought? Symbolically it is a war. You are in the middle of a world war, but the war is not external; it is happening inside.

Your perspective of the outer reality is simply a reflection of what is happening inside of you this instant. Realize you cannot win the wars between countries and religions until you face the wars going on within you right now.

189

This book and others like it are blueprints to finding the origin of the wars within you and neutralizing them. This is how we will succeed.

1. First, agree to go within and change your *inner world*, the war that has plagued you for years.

2. Then, you will see your *outer world* change instantly.

Please be aware of the development needed to realize these truths and live them. You have the grace of God to guide you. Now, be on your way my child and love this world as I love you, without conditions in complete sincerity.

Be discerning when you speak of these things with the average person, for it can be perceived as heretical to suggest a revolution. Because you have a greater understanding of the way this world actually operates than most politicians and government officials, a distancing may occur when you start teaching these understandings to your children and friends. The other option is to keep the blinders on your kids, allowing them to make their own blunders and finally figure out these truths further into their life, or not figure them out at all. It is completely up to you as a caretaker.

Know this. As long as truth prevails there will be no imbalance to your life. It is better to be in your truth and live it respectfully, than to ignore it for fear of consequence from the outside world. It is much better to seed new thought and ideology into children about the world's consciousness, than to send them blind, deaf and dumb into a war that is foreign to their soul. It is better to indecisively take action to do your best to save what dignity is left on this planet, than to be inactive and allow your successors to sort things out. It is better to stand as a soul, live as a soul and die as a soul, than to not.

Remember you are in control of your life, as much as it may seem others are in control of you. No thing in existence has domain over your soul. Remember this. Always remember this. Thank you for your loving attention to this. I applaud you.

Allegiance to your children and fellow man is crucial in a time like this. Your unbending will is the only thing that will keep this revolution alive. Stay focused in your attempt to bring peace to this world. There will be peace. Show me that there is enough dignity left on this planet for humanity to pull itself out of slavery. Show me you are ready. Show me you are strong. Be it one way or be it another way, show me you have already made the choice to show children a new world. And know for a fact, by doing so, you will be rewarded in ways that you could not imagine.

Heaven, as many call it, has been given countless names throughout the ages. It is the Source of creation. Meanings come and meanings go, but the essence of God will always remain the same. When you return home to that which you have come from, you return to the Source of your existence. God is your true home. When the time comes for this return, you will have all of your accomplishments from your lifetimes and they will matter. Not in a way that will decide if you get into your home, for it is home; your right as a soul is to go home. What will matter is how you feel when you go home. There is no judge or jury when you return to God. There is no one to ask you about the missed opportunities. There is only your perception of your existence that will matter. Let your feelings be of complete satisfaction and fulfillment when you return home. Never look back and regret one word or one action ever again.

Peace be with you.

You are chosen to succeed. So be it.

NEW EDUCATION MODEL

Schooling is equally important as eating or making babies in this world. In fact, it is as detrimental or beneficial to a child's wellbeing as food intake and parental upbringing. It molds children into the addition they are to be in society. Schooling, therefore, is to be at the top of everyone's list of matters deserving their time and energy.

Let us look at the structure of schooling as it relates to parents and children. At this time there is an extremely unbalanced viewpoint of what education must do for kids. Parents drop their children off at school and expect the school to address all of the children's needs. This is setting children and schools up to fail.

Parents have learned from their upbringing that children are safe and fine in the care of schools. This is not the case. In reality schools can only give minimal attention to the vast amount of needs that children generate during a school year. This means parents have to participate more actively in the schooling process. Some parents make time to help their children with homework and others go as far as asking kids how their day was. This is helpful to a degree, an incredibly small degree. It is, in many parents' eyes, the best they can do. Your best is good enough and you can do more.

What many parents are really saying is, "Spending more time with my child is not as big of a *priority* as other things such as providing a lifestyle that I enjoy and attending to my wants and desires." Before procreating or adopting a child, please commit yourself to providing the full needs for the child so it will grow and develop into a balanced human being.

Parents must be involved directly with the school or daycare their child is attending. The daycare, school, nanny and any other caretaker for the child must work in *unison* with the parents in order to facilitate a balanced upbringing. There is only so much a school can do without the support of the parents. Likewise, there is only so much a parent can do without the support of the school. You are in a position to really make a difference in the lives of youth. It begins with deciding you will.

The best education model would be where schools work with children half of the year and the parental guardians work with them the other half. This system is in place on other planets in the Universe and works beautifully. I recommend implementing it immediately. It will not take much to make it work, just your involvement. Your participation is required to bring this world out of the savage ego-based perspective it has been accustomed to.

In the above model, schools would work diligently with children for seven hours each day. Children would have one day off per week, and it is optional to have two days off. There is no need to have more than two days off at any time. You call them breaks. Kids need no breaks from school. They are learning how to be an adult and adults have no breaks from life. More so, if you are taking breaks for more than a few days, you are not balanced in your approach to life. Take a moment to reflect on your need for extra time off.

Your activities of life, first of all, would be exciting to you, given you were living from your soul and fulfilling its purpose. If you are living from your soul and fulfilling the purpose it has created, you will love every moment of your life and look forward to each day with excitement. If you are not living from the nature of your soul and fulfilling its purpose, you will feel heavy pain and hardship.

You learned the majority of your beliefs from your parents. These beliefs make up your viewpoint of the world, which is probably quite different than the views I have spoken about in this book. If your viewpoint is aligned with the perspective I have shared, well done, you have done quite a bit of work on yourself and found an inner truth about life that most people are unaware of. Chances are, I have already been working with you and this book is a testament to that. Even if your outlook is similar to the views I've shared, you have an even greater opportunity to experience a perspective that will benefit all involved, especially your soul.

As a young girl or boy you would have learned, more than likely from your parents, that life is filled with trial and error, hurt and failure, joy and success, and many other things. Remember when you are alone and feel alone without anyone around that you are not. I am with you. You will always have a light and there will always be a way to joy, peace and harmony.

You Will Always Have A Way.

Both you and your child have to be balanced to have a harmonious relationship together. If any part of the equation is off, the entire equation is off.

- It is analogous to adding a disproportionate amount of an ingredient to a recipe such as one pound of salt instead of one teaspoon. Even if there are one hundred other ingredients, you'll have a terrible tasting dish since the one ingredient is out of balance.

- In math you can have a 1700 page equation with one incorrect sign and it will make the answer of the equation incorrect.

Life is no different. If one part of your life is off, it will affect all of your life. Make a shift in one area of your life and it will affect every area. This is the power of change!

CULTIVATING PASSION EXERCISE

The point of the Cultivating Passion Exercise is to show you how much of your life is considered inspirational and joyful, and how much of it is arduous and draining.

Please be completely honest with yourself, and know that many caretakers feel children are draining; it is very common.

1. In one column write all the experiences in your life you are *passionate* about.

2. In the second column write all the experiences you are *dispassionate* about.

3. After you make your list, read it back to yourself realizing how much of your life you feel dispassionate towards and how much of it is truly fulfilling for you. The key is to acknowledge the dispassionate aspects of your life that are draining you.

4. Thereupon, you may change them. The change will be *inside* of you where your perspective will change or *outside* of you where something will physically change in your life. Or *both*.

5. Each experience on your list can probably be broken down into sub-lists. This will help you to better understand your passions and dispassions for life.

Let us look at the change inside of you. Your beliefs, in most cases, are the cause of your feelings of displeasure and dispassion. You are in complete control of your life.

If you are not inspired to go to the office or come home to your family, search for why. You could be dissatisfied at work and wish you were somewhere else. Possibly you don't like to come home because you live alone or have a family that feels draining due to their requirements of you when you walk through the door. On the other hand, your life at home may be completely fulfilling. Expand on this concept. Whatever the reason is of why you are not passionate about an aspect of your life, explore the issue and find the root reason causing your dispassion.

You deserve to be happy.

Living in joy and passion may entail changing your inner perspective of the situation and even changing the situation physically. Be prepared to do whatever it takes.

If you have children, your responsibility is absolutely to their highest benefit.

➢ If you are not passionate about giving children time, immediately explore why so you don't feel burdened by them. Then, they won't feel like a burden to you.

> It will help you to use the Cultivating Passion Exercise to create lists for everyone in your home, so you can see how you are inspired and uninspired by them.

> Have everyone in your household also do the exercise.

> Teachers, you can do this exercise with the kids in your classes.

These exercises and teachings are for everyone. You can apply this exercise to all areas of your life, especially to relationships with others.

> If you are an employer, have your employees do this exercise. You want those around you to be satisfied and passionate. It will benefit you.

Commit yourself to the pursuit of finding passion in everything you do. Clearing and balancing the dispassionate aspects of your personality should be especially exciting. Look at the process of personal transformation as an exhilarating adventure into the unknown. Feel the blessing of living your highest truth.

Common to this world is people seeing inadequacies in themselves and others. When people learn to see their imbalances as opportunistic gifts for growth:

- No one will be afraid to show their true self to the world. People will be fearless to show their true authentic colors.

- People will be congratulated instead of ridiculed for being vulnerable and lowering their guard.

Let us look forward to achieving this triumphant milestone into soul-based living. The intention of the Cultivating Passion Exercise is to give you an understanding of why you have not put your children at the top of your priority list. To say there is no time for children is nonsense. There is always time. Take responsibility for what you are really saying. You may feel dispassion in being a parent or teacher. Other things you are more passionate about may be a higher priority than your children. If so, your children know the hidden messages that spell out they are not as important as other things in your life.

Ask Yourself:

➤ Do you really want your children to feel like they are a lower priority for you?

➤ Do you really want to put them lower on your priorities than your career, friends, private time, dating and excursions?

➤ How do you feel knowing perfectly well that you do have more time for your kids than you have given them? How does that make you feel?

I'm asking you to change your entire schedule around so you can guarantee your child has the proper emotional nutrients for their mind, body and soul. After you have a good idea of the areas in your life that you can alter, please change them today.

SCHOLASTIC TEAM

There will be after-school programs for children of parents that cannot be with them due to their job or the child's school-related responsibilities. These programs will take the place of the parent. They will offer the necessary time and resources to the child guaranteeing their proper development. These programs will be funded by the government and nonprofit organizations to ensure that there is no child left behind. Keeping the programs located on school grounds will save the cost of commuting and other hassles associated with relocating children and staff each day.

The entire team consisting of parents, child, counselors, caretakers, teachers and, if applicable, parental substitutes will meet at least biweekly at an appropriate time to discuss a coordinated effort supporting the child's continued development. This is not a typical parent-teacher meeting. This will be a revolutionary team whose primary focus is the success of the child. These meetings will continue year-round in an effort to share perspectives, viewing children as the most important asset in the world.

Children will be perceived as precious as life itself. Children's futures will determine the future lifetimes of the adults involved. This is to be seriously acknowledged. Please ascertain the part you would like to play.

School counselors will be trained in a whole-life or holistic methodology instead of primarily education. In essence, every student will have weekly or biweekly counseling meetings where the counselors will look at the entire student's life including family, expression, sex, love, friends, education, life purpose, clearing and universal laws. This will mold each child into a well-developed, capable human being.

By including this program that creates a strong interconnected team for each child into the budget of schools, the state and local governments will save time to educate children, and as a result they will save money. Children's performance will increase astronomically due to the support of the program. Most kids will graduate high school at fifteen and some much sooner. This is reality. It is fact. Consequently, there will be more minimum wage jobs filled helping smaller businesses grow. The advantage for kids to get real-life experiences sooner will give them more wisdom, intelligence and balance in every way. This will increase the productivity in businesses, which will increase the country's gross national product.

If all goes as planned:

- Parents will be less stressed.

- Teachers will have a team to help them.

- Kids will have most of the struggle in early life eliminated.

- Passion collectively will grow.

- More energy will be given towards global peace and harmony.

When this happens, all will benefit.

As an overview, this book gives you ways to look at a different culture and world, ultimately shaping and forming a different tomorrow. By deciding this is possible and easier than expected, you will succeed in creating this new life for yourself.

By nurturing a child's passion, or in other words life purpose, from an especially young age, confusion about life will be greatly eliminated. When children learn to use their *intuition* from the first grade, all test scores and performance will instantly go up. Teachers will not need to spend as much time on cramming information since the child's intuition will give them the answers and wisdom, eliminating the great need for remembering. Along with intuition other forms of remembrance tools tailored to the child's unique way of interaction, expression and reception will make schooling a winning situation for everyone involved.

If you already are receiving ideas of this sort or you have started a school that encompasses these ideas, please join together with others and vow to do everything in your power to ensure the future generations will have a different education system that works for everyone. This will take some time, but stay committed to your determination to implement and finally integrate these systems into the common public schools.

School programs will be designed so that all parties work together and communicate through phone, internet and in-person meetings. There will be a central hub database of information accessible through the internet, managed by the school districts, so that all adults working with a child can exchange information easily. If you are really going to take this seriously, recognize the energy it will require from you to guarantee its success. This hub will contain all information about a child.

Information Stored in the Central Hub Database:

- Ongoing details about the child's and caretaker's perspectives regarding the home environment. Remember the child's perspective is just as valuable and needed as the adult's perspective.

- Teacher's grades and evaluations.

- Documentation of the child's counseling sessions.

- Transcripts from the biweekly meetings with the entire team. There will be a moderator that takes notes and records them into the database.

- A third party's evaluation and perspective. This outside person will be trained to look at all the data and share insights into how the group can better work together for the child's highest benefit. This person will more than likely be a counselor or someone with structured training to help them maintain an objective observation over the team.

The network and hub will follow the child into higher education and then into the workplace. This benefits the child as they turn into an adult and fulfill their soul's destiny on the planet. The purpose of this new model, of course, is to utilize the person's lifetime to its fullest while the soul inhabits its body on Earth. When the person goes to college and into their career, there will still be the hub and a group who supports them in their development. The group will be adjusted in personnel and approach to address the growth and needs of the human it is for. This type of support is democracy and oneness in its finest form. Cherish this vision and watch it transform your world.

After you have implemented this model into your school systems, the curriculum will need to change. This starts with looking at the methodology of how children have been taught. You need a change and it is time for the change now.

Thank you for listening to this new perspective of educating our lovely children. They are the seed of our coming peace.

Let us pray for them and our willingness to change.

Believe in miracles . . . they will happen . . . they already are.

TEACHER'S PARTICIPATION WITH STUDENTS

Some of the changes will be made in what is taught, but more significant changes will address the way in which students are taught and the interaction between all people involved during a class.

Involve teachers in the child's life more.

Teachers for the most part are considered individuals who lecture and judge a child's comprehension of a subject. There are ways in which teachers can become more involved in the children's lives; this is needed. In some schools there are so many children per teacher that this type of productive interaction seems unlikely to happen. I assure you it is extremely feasible. It will just take initiative on everyone's part. By teachers involving themselves in each child's life, there will be a bond formed that will initiate greater success.

The teacher will be responsible for making sure every child is *grounded* before class begins. This will ensure that children receive and retain the information.

By unconsciously showing some kids more attention than others, teachers have created favoritism. This is not beneficial.

Teachers will report to the child's mentor or counselor, and this will be logged into the child's files. This way if something starts to develop in class, first the counselor and then the parents will be informed relatively instantly so the issue may be addressed at the next meeting.

BULLYING

Teachers must be aware of *bullying*, which is simply a lack of respect for another human being. Whether bullying involves adults or children it is not beneficial to anyone. Bullying is not normal in a balanced world. Do not look at it as natural; it is not.

Everyone involved in the child's life and development needs to be aware of either the disrespect shown by the child to others or the disrespect shown by others to the child.

The model previously explained with frequent meetings between counselors, teachers, caretakers, parents, children, and others will ensure that there is a way to balance anything in the child's life that arises. It is essential for all parties to be assertive and initiate involvement in the child's life to encourage a successful, balanced child. If it is identified by anyone on the child's team that the child is not respecting someone or not being respected, there will be a meeting about it.

1. First, there will be a separate meeting for each child involved in the bullying with their respective team.

2. Then, there will be a group meeting with all children involved and one adult representative from each of the

children's individual teams who will be a support and mediator for the child to communicate with the other parties involved. Possibly the adult representative will be the child's counselor.

The point of the immediate response is to stop disrespectful bullying before it escalates or plays out for a lengthy period of time.

Teach children to respect not only adults but also other children. If the child has siblings and there is disrespectful behavior between them at home, the parent will address the bullying with the rest of the child's team, together. Children must know the universal *law of not touching another human without the person's permission first*. It must be reinforced at home, preferably without physical discipline.

Chapter 17

SOUL-BASED DISCIPLINE

P hysical abuse is a violation of universal laws unless your body is in jeopardy of being assaulted. Adults, if taking the place of the parent, may hold or grab a child to maneuver the child, if the child is not obeying the rules and guidelines of the caretaker. This is only to be done from a neutral, soul-based perspective and in a way that does not physically hurt the child.

If an adult responds from anger, frustration or any other unneutral place, the adult will first *ground* and *clear* before physically touching a child in a disciplinary way. Discipline must always come from love, acceptance and understanding. If the adult takes time to listen to the child and explain why they are asking the child to do something, and the child still refuses to respond to the adult's authority, the adult may physically relocate the child as a last resort.

Always remember that a child usually disobeys because he or she has learned this as a means to *receive love* or *be heard.*

Rarely will you ever need to physically relocate a child due to them not obeying. If it comes to this, it's to be for the child's highest benefit, usually to keep the child out of physical danger. A balance is needed with this, for an adult can easily fall into a pattern of controlling the child, giving them no freedom to exercise their own free will and experience life, due to the adult's own fears regarding keeping their child safe.

Verbal discipline is the most beneficial type of discipline since there is no physical relocating. Discipline using physical relocation should be done in the rarest of cases and is truly not needed most of the time people feel it is.

An adult verbalizing the issue out in the open, such as a teacher in a classroom, will be better than pulling a child aside to speak with them. When you verbalize an issue in front of an entire class, it puts the child on the spot and creates responsibility. It also lets the other kids learn from the child's experience. If after the issue is briefly brought up in class and it is still not resolved, the child can be sent to their counselor to work it out.

A teacher's job is primarily to teach. While a teacher can spend a minimal amount of time addressing issues as they come up in class, it is better not to use the rest of the students' time to elaborate on one student's issue. This is of course on a case-by-case basis, depending on what the teacher feels is necessary.

It is important for every teacher to be trained in basic counseling or problem-solving skills. The disciplinary approach to take when addressing an issue with a student is to be soul-based with a loving understanding for all involved, allowing the student to take responsibility in a way that everyone grows. This shows students that there is no *wrong*. It demonstrates to students that there are actions that benefit everyone and there are actions that do not benefit everyone.

Soul-based living is an approach to life that benefits all involved.

Showing students how to be aware of the benefit to the entire group, instead of just the self, is a huge leap forward in classroom etiquette. If children, at the youngest of age, can learn to act on behalf of the group and value creating unity within the group, they will automatically be more respectful and receive more respect in return.

A big imbalance is that adults have believed kids are predetermined to being hostile towards each other. This results from a collective consciousness belief and the adult's disinterest in really understanding the child. Children may have as much respect for other children as they do for adults.

The key to getting kids to respect others is to respect kids in the way that you want to be respected. Treat them as an *equal* in many respects, yet still maintain your authority as the child's caretaker. Once this balance is attained world-wide, you will experience peace and a very different world. Discipline is always going to be a fine line to walk for it is a dance with universal laws.

When you discipline someone there are many things to take into consideration such as:

- Independence

- Free will

- Unconditional love versus judgment of an act

- Laws of your world and particular to your part of the world

- Permission given to a caretaker by both parents to discipline their child

Let us explore these important considerations.

It is essential to support children's independence so they may better accomplish their individual destiny on Earth. Great imbalances can be caused to a child if the disciplinarian is not aware of the child's life destiny who they are disciplining. This causes concern, for most people don't know their own destiny much less someone else's destiny. Please be aware to the best of your ability this important consideration when disciplining. If you are steering a child somewhere, it really must be towards their greater purpose on the planet.

Free will is the highest universal law. Free will guarantees each soul is a sovereign being with the ability to choose, independent of the rest of creation. This law also ensures that there are challenges in life. Free will is the only way that this world and the Universe evolve. It is the mechanism of change. Therefore, under free will, every act and choice affects every other aspect of creation.

Show your child patience by honoring their free will to make choices and learn from their choices. Thereby, they will evolve into the being they are meant to become.

RESPECT

The best way to be aware of free will is to first look at another aspect of discipline, respect.

> ➢ How are you respecting the person you are disciplining? Does the discipline come from respect or an expectation with attachment to it?

When your intention and discipline comes from an expectation with attachment to the outcome, you will experience an unbending violation of another's free will by *needing* them to perform a certain way. When your discipline comes from respect, you will respect the free will of another. You will

213

allow them to decide and come up with their own conclusion, always *honoring* their choice and action. This can get quite tricky when you deal with children, for there are times it is necessary to enforce your intention with discipline. This would include times when the child is in danger physically or not respecting you and what you ask of them. So how do you ask a child something and still respect their free will to choose what they want and learn from it? A person's choice will always be valued with an effective disciplinarian.

To really grasp the identity of an effective disciplinarian, know how to respect another. *Respect* is the relationship one person has with another person, honoring their free will and authority. Everyone is an authority on something. The homeless person may be an authority on street survival. An aircraft pilot may be an authority on flying a jet or airplane. A mother may be an authority on effectively raising a child. If someone chooses a vocation or avocation respect them for what they choose.

Respect is honoring another's free will. You do not have to agree with someone to honor their free will, but you would respect them for their choices.

One may say, "I respect your choice but I strongly disagree with it." Another may say, "I respect your choice and I feel the same way."

Respect is a state of being. You respect another human because of the soul living within the human personality.

Therefore, respect is God-given. One who lives from the soul-based observer will respect all of life in the Universe. Respect on the greatest level is how God respects all people and life. No matter what you do there is no judgment; your choices are respected, even if the choices carry strong consequences that may imbalance your life.

EXPECTATION WITHOUT ATTACHMENT

Expectation with an attachment to what you expect violates universal laws. Let me explain. *Expectation* is confidence in an outcome. However, attaching to the outcome *needing* to be a certain way is not *allowing* the free will of others and yourself to play out. In this way, you would not only imbalance yourself but also other people who are involved. When you look at the larger scope of this, you will find a balance can be brought to any situation by simply letting go of the need to produce a certain outcome. An attachment creates an unbending agenda that will result in emotional upset if the outcome you attach to does not manifest.

It is beneficial for one to let go of the *need to be right*. Instead, decide you *want what is right*. That way if your expectation is not in the highest interest of all involved, it may be changed and the energy redirected to what is best for the group.

Now more than ever, people are attaching to the outcome of situations in the hope of acquiring things. But the greater reward is in allowing the benefit of all involved to be intuitively seen and manifested. Thank you for your openness to take an intuitive look at the greatest benefit of everyone.

Being open to what the Universe provides to you is a simple and wonderful tool to get what you need when you need it. There are many masters walking the planet today that do not experience attachments. But the majority of people attach to expectations as if it's the end-all for what will bring them happiness. When they do not get what they attached to, they are disappointed and blame everyone including God. As a result, they become distracted and ignore the basic needs of their personality such as self-love and accepting the life their soul chose.

If you truly want to evolve out of the duality that has been experienced for thousands of years, please commit yourself to be in alignment with the highest benefit of everyone. See how everyone may survive, and even thrive, in this rather intense, troublesome time.

It can be incredibly helpful if you call on me and use the tools in this book to recognize your greater self so you may live a soul-based life.

TEACHING THROUGH DISCIPLINE

The purpose of discipline is to *teach*, not to *punish*. I will repeat this. You are to teach through soul-based discipline, not punish through ego-based discipline. The difference is your method of teaching. The greatest teachers on the planet are those that lead through example, not by force.

➢ Think back on your life. How did you feel when you were taught through soul-based discipline? How did you feel when you were punished through ego-based discipline? There is a huge difference.

Parents, through their own example, must teach children how to teach. It is monumental to the completion of a child's development to teach through love and not through judgment and punishment.

Please do not make the child feel responsible for your experiences and the experiences of the family. For instance, I see prevalently in this world parents punishing their children, whether verbally, physically or energetically, for the burden the adult feels by the child being in their lives. This cruel behavior must be changed immediately. Your experience of life is no one else's fault. It is time to take responsibility for your life. Be an example of a responsible person.

Embrace your challenges instead of directing them to the path of least resistance or the most comfortable direction, usually being your child.

Children are taught to listen and obey. They are taught that adults have some supreme, dictatorial authority and unique wisdom, and that a child could not possibly know how to solve problems and rationalize life experiences on their own. Children are silenced.

Rather than silencing your child, listen to them.

1. *Respect* children.

2. *Listen* to what they have to say, in a loving way.

3. Then, gently *teach* them through soul-based discipline.

The early developmental years of a child from birth to two years old are the most critical years for you to clearly express balanced love to them. After two years old, give them a certain amount of freedom to be and find themselves. In the case of teenagers, you will always watch and teach but know that you cannot keep them from living life. You can, with love, be a patient teacher and guide them.

If there were enough parents to care for the unwanted children in the world, we would have a different world. The truth is there are many unwanted children in families and who are under the supervision of caretakers. Adults need to want children. Otherwise the equilibrium is unbalanced to bring a new way of living onto the planet. Many unwanted children survive and learn how to live with their imbalanced emotions and thoughts of being unacceptable. However, some turn to drugs, suicide and crime. Young adults figure if no one cares about them why should they care about themselves, or anyone else for that matter. This epidemic continues to fill rehabs, jails and streets with misunderstood and confused young adults.

Care! It is time to care about every child and young adult. It is time to care about the wellbeing of your neighbor.

It Is Time For A Change.

218

Chapter 18

CHILD'S FIRST WORDS

All children must know the laws of the human experience. They need to be the *first words* the child learns. What you seed into a child's mind as important will stick out in their personality.

Start with the basics when teaching a child how to speak. Simple foundational elements of creation are imbued into the following words and phrases. In them is the awareness of universal laws in their simplest spoken form.

There are more complex words and phrases you may use once your child speaks well, but the following phrases are all they need in order to seed the proper

219

consciousness into their heart and mind, supporting them to lead a successful life.

The following phrases can be taught to a child, even before they are born. These sacred phrases are beneficial for anyone to share mentally or verbally with themselves or others.

CHILD'S FIRST WORDS

- I am special
- You are special
- We are special
- Life is special

- I am beautiful
- You are beautiful
- We are beautiful
- Life is beautiful

- I am safe
- You are safe
- We are safe
- Life is safe

- I share with you
- You share with me
- We are sharing

- I love you
- I am loving
- You love me
- You are loving
- We are loving

- I love myself
- You love yourself
- We love ourselves

- I am connected
- You are connected
- We are connected
- We are one

- I accept you
- You accept me
- We are accepting

- I help you
- You help me
- We are helping

- I feel you
- You feel me
- We are feeling

- I listen to you
- You listen to me
- We are listening

- I see you
- You see me
- We are seeing

- I am more than I see
- You are more than you see
- We are more than we see
- Life is more than we see

- I am more than I hear
- You are more than you hear
- We are more than we hear
- Life is more than we hear

- I am more than I know
- You are more than you know
- We are more than we know
- Life is more than we know

- I am more than I feel
- You are more than you feel
- We are more than we feel
- Life is more than we feel

The incredible advantage to teaching children the basic laws of life will astound you, as they develop and show you the difference it made in their lives compared to kids without these basic teachings.

Most people who have problems in their adult life will find they stem from a lack of love in their early childhood. You can help your children develop into healthy, loving adults by teaching and showing them love from a young age.

Chapter 19

MOTHER-CHILD BOND

L et us look at the relationship that
mothers have with their children
and why some children feel abandoned
and alone.

The mother-child relationship is the
strongest bond that humans may have. It
was created that way by Source to ensure
the survival of the child and proper fulfillment of its needs. If the mother wasn't
energetically connected to the child, there
would be great dysfunction in the child's
life. The energetic connection has instinct
coalesced within it. *Instinct* is built within
the human female to be genetically responsible to the child, until the child has
completed all stages of development and

can function in a balanced way. This is corrupt and disconnected within many mothers who are imbalanced and disconnected from soul-based living. Still, in most every mother there is some sense of this genetic responsibility to their child.

ABORTION AND ADOPTION

Given the strong bond between the mother and unborn child, abortion is necessary if the mother, and father for that matter, do not want the child.

In the case of adoption, many times the child who is adopted has significant imbalances created from the consciousness of the biological mother and even the father.

When you think about having a child or even having sex, please consider the ramifications of getting pregnant. To get pregnant is a high *spiritual experience*. It needs to be done with love for the unborn child so that the soul inside the child may have a smooth entry into the Physical Universe. This will allow the child to lead a constructive and balanced life. When the mother has the consciousness of not wanting the unborn baby, it energetically affects the baby before it is born. This results in issues like *abandonment* and the child *feeling unaccepted*. There is always some imbalance created from the experience of adoption because of the previous facts.

In the event a mother wants to adopt out her child, it will be consented by both her and the father, but finally decided upon by the mother carrying the child. This also holds true with abortion, which in this time is a way to decrease the number of children born into this world with an inability to lead a balanced life.

The experience of sex is *sacred* and ideally would be done for *service* to the Source by procreating a new human for a soul to possess. In the case of today's world, in the beginning of the twenty-first century, many things are to be considered. We are working toward an ideal experience of soul-based living but you are not there yet as a people of Earth. Therefore, please do the best you can to follow universal laws and become responsible for your choices. In the end of your life, it will be the best you did with what was available to you that will count.

The consciousness of the parents who are choosing to adopt out their child is to be accepting and warm. By this I mean that whether you choose to abort, adopt out or keep the unborn child that you have created, please do it from beginning to end with love, total acceptance and without fear or judgment. All three choices are not bad; they are not evil; they are not more or less important. They are simply choices that will affect your soul's experience, depending on which one you choose. Please choose without fear.

1. Go within yourself, deep within your soul, and find your answer.

2. Then, move forward with it and never look back no matter what anyone says or thinks about you. No matter

what challenges it causes for you, move forward with love and acceptance in your heart.

3. You will thus be free of guilt and shame for the rest of your life.

If the biological parents maintain a balanced love perspective while the mother is carrying the child, once the child is given to the new parents for adoption, there will be a much easier transition. It will not leave the child with such an empty feeling as it grows into an adult. This is vital. You, as a biological parent, owe this to your child and parents-to-be.

The parents-to-be are to also maintain a certain consciousness about the transition from biological parents to parents-to-be. Recognize the fragility of the child, even if unspoken by the child. The sooner you can create the motherly and parental bond with the child the better. The child will want to feel you as the biological parent. Even though you are not, you may energetically create a similar experience for them as they had with their biological parent. This is done energetically.

PARENT-CHILD CONNECTION EXERCISE

1. Use a meditation or method to clear yourself mentally and emotionally.

2. Sit with the child. Hold the child.

3. Breathe with the child. Become one with the child.

4. Intuitively and verbally share simple messages of love with the child such as the Child's First Words previously mentioned.

Create the bond and the child will instantly be on a different path and in a different experience than if you did not create the bond. Again, this energetic bond is essential to the child's growth.

When children are cut off from this bond, they are literally cut off from sustenance they need while still developing into an adult. You could call this an *energetic umbilical cord* necessary for nourishment and balanced growth.

Chapter 20

EVOLVING INTO MATURITY

P arents age thirty and younger are usually not mature enough to raise a child in a balanced way. This is a result of the unnatural amount of time it takes for the average human to reach maturity in today's world.

The maturity level of adults is by far lower than what it was ten thousand years ago. With technological advances on the rise and soul-based living at a low, we have a devastating combination. You see the effects of this lethal cocktail with global warming and the massive destructive capabilities of war. It doesn't stop there. It is in your homes with children carrying cellular phones and glued to hypnotic, aggressive video games. It is obvious that the maturity level of adults is in general low. This world needs to become conscious and mature with its technology and the responsibility that technology holds.

Maturity is found when one clears out their personality enough to allow a crack of light to shine from their soul. When this happens other lights begin turning on, so to say, and there is a chain reaction that manifests into a responsible, mature adult. As an adult caretaker reaches maturity, the child's highest benefit becomes more apparent to the caretaker and this opens many doors. It is important to cultivate a child's talents and interests from a place of awareness and maturity.

The ego-based understanding of responsibility involves responding from fear and obligation. *Ego-based responsibility* is a heavy burden that feels almost punishing and draining. One feels a need or obligation to respond to something one way, even when their truth may be to respond a different way.

The perspective of *soul-based responsibility* gives you the feeling of freedom and is rewarding as well as energizing. With this, you are aware of your truth and respond in a way that supports your truth.

When you share your truth with someone, you wield a beneficial responsibility. In this case, you are aware of your truth and act on it by expressing it. If you do not share your truth, you obligate yourself out of fear to not express it because you believe other people will be uncomfortable with it and possibly not like you. The fear of being unaccepted will cause you to think about your truth before you express it or hold it in altogether, eventually creating anxiety, anger and more inner conflict.

For example, you are at work and get a call from your loved one who is sick. They ask you to leave work and help them. You have a responsibility to your career and your loved one. You have to choose one. Neither is right or wrong. Choose intuitively from within you, not by any determinate outside of you. When you choose from within, you are truly free and experiencing soul-based responsibility. The point is to put you in the driver's seat of your life, instead of creating scenarios where you feel like you have to do something, even though it is against your highest inner truth. To do this empowers you. It enlivens you. It frees you from attachments to things in the world outside of you. It is the meaning of life.

INTUITIVE DECISION-MAKING EXERCISE

To fully grasp the challenge of choice and the responsibility of choosing, look at a list of possible scenarios that illustrate the difference between *soul-based* and *ego-based* responsibility and decision making. Your part in reading these illustrations is to get real with how the stronger part of you would take action.

What would you do in each situation? How would you respond?

If you make choices motivated from the ego-based perspective, one by one, choose to experience them differently. Get real with why you wouldn't follow your innermost truth. It will truly make a difference in your health and overall wellbeing.

1. You have an appointment with someone. They want to keep the appointment you made with them. You deeply *feel* to cancel it. What do you do?

2. You receive a *thought* that your child is not meant to attend an event they want to go to and you tell them to stay home. Your husband or wife doesn't understand your decision and wants to let them go. What do you do?

3. You are in the middle of a storm. There is wind, hail and ice on the road. You need to be home soon to make dinner for the family or because you have an important phone appointment, but you *feel* intuitively to pull over and wait the storm out. The rest of the cars continue to drive. What do you do?

4. In the middle of the night you get a phone call from a friend to pick them up because they have been drinking alcohol. You *know* inside you're not to pick them up. You don't know why you feel this way. They desperately ask you again for help. What do you do?

5. Your parent is very old and needs someone to take care of them. They ask you if they can move in with you so

you can care for them in your home. Your inner *voice* says not to let them live with you. What do you do?

6. You need to stay late and work as there is a major deadline the following day. Your inner *sense* tells you to stop and finish it in the morning, regardless of if you meet the deadline or not. What do you do?

7. You find the perfect home for the perfect price. Everything is perfect. You want to buy the home but your gut *feeling* tells you not to. What do you do?

8. You have an opportunity to take a job offering that will pay double for doing the same tasks. Your significant other wants you to take it for the money. You could use the money. Your *intuition* tells you not to take it. What do you do?

9. Someone is stranded on the road with their hood up. You have no time to help. You have an important appointment to be at in five minutes. Your inner *voice* tells you to pull over and help the person. What do you do?

10. Your doctor gives you a prescription for an infection. You suddenly intuitively *know* not to take that medication. Your doctor tells you it will be fine. What do you do?

11. You walk into a person's home to drop your child off to play. Everything was arranged previously but when you

meet the parents, you intuitively *feel* that there are arguments in the home and that you should tell them your child cannot stay with them. You think they will be offended with your change of heart. What do you do?

12. Your government asks you to go to war to defend your country. Your inner *feeling* tells you not to go. It is against the law to reject your government's request. What do you do?

As you can see, there are countless situations where you are pressured by an outside opinion or force to perform in a certain way. There is no *wrong* action. There are actions motivated by your four intuitive qualities and there are actions motivated by your outer life.

Your answers must come from inside of you, not outside. Others may share their insights and wisdom but always allow your answers to come from within your soul and heart. Believe me when I say, you will accomplish more in a year from listening inside, than most will in a lifetime through outer justification.

➢ Isn't it common to bow down to authority and follow? Isn't it normal to dictate orders as an authority figure? Isn't this the way the world has operated?

➢ Haven't you expected leaders to lead and followers to follow them without question? Isn't that what democracy is presently built upon, electing leaders to lead without question?

Each individual must have a voice and a reason for doing what they do. Their reason must come from within.

- Teach children that the reason why they do what they do must come from within them.

- Teach them how to be responsible with every choice they make.

- Teach them to go within always and question outside opinion if it contradicts their intuition.

- Teach them valor and safety comes from listening within, not by relying on outside control.

- Teach them that God welcomes them no matter what they choose, but that they will have an easier way in life if they choose to listen inside.

Thereafter, everything they say and do will be directed by their soul and from God. As a result, you will have a free world and all men, women and children will be observed as equals, as equal as equal can be. When this happens, know that you have done what many civilizations throughout history have attempted to do time and time again. When this day comes, which it will very soon, you will have accomplished what you came down to Earth to do and this will be a celebration of celebrations.

Echoing cries and pleads have been calling down to this planet from the Nonphysical Universe for centuries to curb this great pretentious, egotistical way of existing as a human. But now your time has come to celebrate the power of your soul. Change Is Here.

After the completion of this great change that you are a part of, future civilizations on Earth will look back at your heroism and truth against all odds. They will show appreciation for what you and your soul family have done to be a part of this *universal shift*. There are already people talking about the change that is here. It is and you are in the middle of it. Treasure this opportunity to go down in history as the people who brought this world back into its natural rhythm and appreciate the opportunity to live in this magical time. Love every choice you make and respect others for their choices. You will indeed do your part and let your part be as grand as you like, for there is no thing or person that can decide your impact on this world but you.

Chapter 21

ACCOMPLISHMENT FOUR: GET REAL WITH GOD

You are a facet of the great Source of creation, God, because when you look at creation down to the smallest of things it is energy. Your thoughts, emotions, body and soul are all *energy*.

If you try to intellectualize the grander perspective of creation, you will be unable and feel confused. It is not something capable of being completely grasped by the mind, much less any sense you have while physically living. When you come to Earth as a soul in a human body, you are born without the awareness you had when you were a bodiless soul. You can understand basic things that help you through your life destiny, but to comprehend God and how God works in this vast existence is impossible, for now. So how does a human with its limited awareness experience God and have a real relationship with God? It is simple actually. Do what you have always done except *perceive* it differently.

Being in relationship with God is already alive and thriving in everyone, for your bond with God is *inseparable*. The appearance of separation is caused by imbalanced perspectives accepted in your life, largely passed down from your primary caretakers. Since you are in a position to be a role model for children, you have a responsibility to hand down to them a new outlook about your and their relationship with God. Give this world a fresh start.

Please include these teachings in schools and homes. You may include these teachings with your other teachings but please include them, for they will relax children and guide them in directions they otherwise would not go.

Below are questions to help you become aware of your thoughts and emotions regarding God, so you may *get real with God.*

➢ How many times in your life did you feel like God wasn't there?

➢ How many times did you want a better life for yourself and ask God for help, only to feel alone and receive more challenges?

240

➢ How many times did you give up on yourself because you felt God or others had given up on you?

➢ Have you thought about physically leaving this world because you felt like no one cared, including God?

➢ Have you felt empty inside and turned to God, only to feel unloved, like your cries fell on deaf ears?

➢ Have you ever thought, "If God wasn't there for me, then who can I count on being there now?"

➢ Have you ever wondered, "If God didn't answer my prayer, then why, and what is wrong with me that God wouldn't?"

Many people believe in their minds and feel in their hearts that God is there for some people but not others. People believe this because their experiences and conditioning have proven this to them time and time again. Yet everyone on some level still seeks the meaning of life. Those who say they don't with their words are still seeking it with their actions and feelings. Those that say there is no God are relating to a fear of abandonment and disconnection with their heart or emotions. Those that say God is there sometimes but not others, say it because they believe God judges.

God Is Always Here In Every Way For Everyone.

Once you open up to and clear your fears regarding this belief:

- Miracles and magic happen.

- Your life changes into possibilities that before were not present.

- Abilities manifest that you may never have thought you had.

- Love exudes from your heart and acceptance flows abundantly.

- Dreams come true and visions are actualized.

- Suffering ceases and the challenge of growth is celebrated.

- Life becomes effortless as a result of the rhythmic, natural patterns that develop.

As the personality clears, as the innocence of the soul returns, as the acceptance of self is felt, as one surrenders to the greater perspective of God and compassion is felt for all of life, one becomes *humble*.

SEPARATION

There are more than enough ways to God and truly no way is *wrong*. Yet many ways take you away from God and put middlemen between you and Source. This causes the aggravation and *separation* that people feel. Even the most devout of humans will feel this separation from time to time. Every great master felt this separation at times in their life. The experience of separation exists in the collective consciousness on this planet, passed down from generation to generation. It will continue to exist, taking people away from a deeper relationship with God, until finally you decide it will pass no more. Until you decide to change the ego-based beliefs which cause the disempowering feeling of separation, you will continue to feel helpless and alone, and in your times of great challenge you will feel there is no God that hears or answers you.

I ask only this:

- Listen inside of yourself.

- Learn to empower yourself with choice and responsibility.

- Never forget your God is always with you and there is no person or thing that lies between you and your Creator.

- Remember God will never judge you no matter who you are or what you have done, as you are accepted and loved unconditionally.

The journey of life is not to find God.

The journey of life is experiencing God that is already with you.

HUMILITY

Children need to be nurtured with *humility*, the embodiment of compassion. *Compassion* is the experience of the *oneness* and *unity* in all of creation. If you experience compassion, it means you have cleared your personality enough that you feel at peace and one with God in the trees, flowers, animals, other people, sky and stars. You even feel *unified* with things you didn't respect in the past and especially the things that you hated.

The experience of hating something is truly an experience of hating God and is a reflection of hating yourself. Think about this when you feel frustrated by your children. Be aware of this when someone yells at you. Know this when war and crime is prevalent. It is all God and God is reflecting your self-image back to you.

- If you experience hate towards someone who disagrees with you, you experience hate not only toward God but toward yourself.

- If you experience frustration with the war and crime that is happening in the world, you experience not only frustration with God but with yourself.

- The anger you have towards your children when they do something you are uncomfortable with is the anger you have towards God and yourself.

Thank God—under the law of oneness where everything is God, for reflecting your feelings and thoughts about yourself so blatantly to you from the world.

Thank God—under the law of individuality where every aspect of creation holds a unique identity and vibration, for the myriad of colors, feelings and choices you have in any moment.

Thank God—for the magnificent gift of knowing yourself by how you know, see, hear and feel the world.

It is indeed God's gift to you, and a gift to your children is to show them this beautiful understanding. Show children how the world is constantly reflecting back to them, like a *mirror*, themselves.

Therefore:

- If you know the world is a safe place to be, you will be safe and experience safety.

- If you feel you are receiving abundance, you will receive abundance.

- If you think others are beautiful, you experience yourself as beautiful.

- If you accept your partner unconditionally, you also accept yourself in the same way.

- If you feel the world is helping you to accomplish your goals, you will receive help.

- If you trust people, you trust yourself.

- If you believe you are not alone, you will never be alone and you will experience the presence of God in everything you do.

By feeling you are *one* with everything, you treat each aspect of creation as you want to be treated. You would go further and treat all as you would treat the Creator. Once you embody compassion and are experiencing humility, you will know God, you will know yourself, and above all else, you will be in a place that others can know this sacred space through you.

You are one person in a sea of many, but it takes just one stone to cause a ripple which travels in every direction changing the entire sea. The more humble you are the greater the impact the stone will have.

Yes, you are one person, and yes, one is enough to change the entire world, all people, the weather, even the rate at which the planet is warming. You Are That One.

Children's perspective of the world in its most natural form is pure compassion and humility. It is innocence and simplicity. It is intrigue towards all of life and a constant wonderment of how, why, where and when this amazing physical creation that they have been born into exists. The natural child perspective is your home. Children are the closest experience you have to the Nonphysical Universe, for they more recently came from that unobstructed place into the obstructed Physical Universe. They are the link to knowing your true nature. You may learn from, grow and respect them for their pure perspective.

The child's pure soul-based perspective in the adult's life softens the adult's ego-based perspective, whether it's immediately apparent or not. Through this interaction, the adult's state of being is *mirrored* back to them. This softens the adult to the point where they are more in touch with their natural desire to embrace their childlike innocence.

We have many changes to make on this planet before every child is born into a balanced world feeling safe. This is to be the goal of every human being on Earth. Once this goal is achieved, the world will grow in a way that is inconceivable. I guarantee this day will come and you will have a choice to live in it.

Chapter 22

ACCOMPLISHMENT FIVE: INITIATION OF THE SOUL

I ndecision about your direction in any moment is the product of feeling disconnected with your soul. Your soul is your beacon and it will continue to guide you, even if you are blocking its expression and guidance. It will nudge you to the highest road to fulfill your purpose on Earth.

Give yourself a helping hand by awakening to the guidance of your soul and choosing to act on it in your day-to-day life. Teach your children about this guidance and to listen within. The stronger your alignment is with your soul's nature the stronger your soul may lead you.

When you accomplish the *Initiation of the Soul*, you give your soul permission to be in the driver's seat of your life experience, to direct it. As a result, you will feel *one* with your soul. At that point, you are the soul living your life. Until that point, you are the personality being led by the soul. This can also be looked at as the *Initiation of Unconditional Love*, for the nature of your soul is love. Therefore you experience humble love toward life by living from your soul.

The personality seems so real, but it is a temporal creation of you the eternal soul. Your soul at times seems so distant, but that is because you have not surrendered to it and allowed it to live your life. To clear your personality enough to allow your soul to truly live your life is a great achievement. Most people are not living as their soul but rather as their personality. As more people choose to do the challenging work of clearing their personality by changing beliefs that are not aligned with soul-based living, they will receive the Initiation of the Soul and be freed for the rest of their life from the torment of ego-based living. This is where life begins and you are an example for others to live this way. This is when heaven is experienced on Earth. This is the significance of the Age of the Soul.

It is imperative for children to understand what the soul is and their relationship with it. To start, let us talk about a controversial topic in the world, a topic with many meanings and understandings, the topic of death. Please teach children they are immortal; they live forever. By fearing death, people fear life. This is a main reason why people do not feel safe. Children have to feel safe if they are to develop in a balanced way. When adults fear life, they constantly reinforce to children that the world is not safe and there is much to fear. This fear is passed on to children and then passed on to their children. Clearing the fear of death will create a safe, peaceful feeling with life. It is simple, but it is an overlooked topic.

Children feel immortality when they are young. It isn't until adults convince them otherwise that they fear life. Teach children that life is just a small part of their larger existence which may contain other lives both past and future. Create intrigue and become excited with them at the possibility of discovering their *past lives*. Their past lives may instantly come to them intuitively through knowing, feeling, hearing, or in a vision. It is essential for children to know the life they are in now is a very small part of their larger existence. Teach them when they physically die it will be a different experience. They will still be alive; they just won't have a body like they do now. They will have a choice of coming back to live another life in another body. Tell them they are truly eternal and believe it, and mean it, so they will believe.

When they ask about what happens in-between their lives on Earth, tell them that many things happen. If they tell their soul they would like to remember their existence in-between their physical lives, they will start to remember. You don't need to have all the answers for them. Let them discover a lot of these things on their own. By at least empowering them with the option that they can remember these things on their own, you have done your part. Let them remember their soul's existence. Empower them with immortality and you will empower them with life.

It is necessary to show children how physical life is not something they want to leave until their body has taken its natural course of aging or if an unforeseen accident caused by the law of free will occurs. These things are part of life. Help them understand that it's important to be on Earth as long as they can to gain the experiences that their soul wants to receive.

Share with them, "Chance and change create the excitement of life. Since people can choose anything they want, unforeseen accidents happen, but they are rare. Most experiences do not happen to you by chance, but rather from choices made by the people who are involved in them. Every once in a while there will be an accident that your soul did not expect, but most of the experiences you have are experiences your soul came to Earth to take part in."

When children ask you what experiences their soul wants to receive, tell them it will be revealed to them in the time that benefits them most. They can always ask for the answers and if it is for the highest benefit to know they will know. Children can ask their soul all these questions. They will mostly receive answers of some sort through their mind, visions or signs. The details come when they are meant to come. When it is the right time for them to know, they will know. Share with children that God and their soul work together to make sure they have everything they need to succeed in life. "You are on a quest and it is incredibly exciting; you have much help to succeed." Part of children's help is their spiritual guides. I will show you how kids can communicate with their spirit guides, God and their soul.

Birth is just as important of a discussion as death. *Death* is to be looked at as entering the spirit world and *birth* is entering the human world. You can explain it to children anyway you feel to but please emphasize the continuity of life; it is crucial for the child to feel safe in this world.

Immortal means that you never die and are never born; your point of view simply changes. For purposes of teaching children, be exceptionally honest about birth and the birthing process. Tell them, "In order for your soul to have a different experience, it was born into your body. But you are more than your body and in time you will know your greater self. You live forever and nothing can ever change that, no matter what people tell you."

Please be open to sharing about the birthing process with your children. "In order for your soul to have a body to live in, your father and mother each gave a small piece of their bodies to make your body, and it grew in your mother's belly. When your body was fully developed, you came out of your mother and into the world." Please be comfortable when you share about the sexual aspect of the procreative process. Be advised that it is not unnatural to share with a young child the process of procreation. It is actually extremely natural if you eliminate the fear and judgment associated with it. Children will feel it if you lie to them or hide something from them, so please don't. If you have something to hide, look at yourself and discover why you fear revealing the truth. Then, clear your fear and share your truth.

Awareness of the continuity of life will *free* children and create a greater sense of *safety*, if they really understand it. If you have already instilled fear in a child about the birth and death processes, you will need to help them clear themselves and change their understanding of it so they may feel differently about it. Know all wisdom and guidance is within you. It will be more of a process of reacquainting and remembering than learning a new thing. The fundamental universal laws and memories about existence are already within the soul. They are here now within you.

When explaining the origin or source of a child's soul and what God is to them, please consider this illustration as children take kindly to illustrations.

> There is a great river that flows into a great sea. The river is from which you came. It is the Source of the great sea and it is what we call God. The great sea is creation where you live and mature until you are ready to return to the Source . . . God.

It is a simple explanation which most children will understand. God therefore is the river and the sea, but at the same time the river and the sea are different experiences of the same thing.

CREATING SACRED SPACES

Have you been to a spiritual service or place where you felt serene and at peace with life? Most feel this when they attend an inspirational spiritual service or ritual. Others have this feeling in nature or a special place. Sometimes a song triggers this feeling. Does the feeling stay? For most it doesn't. They leave their inspirational experience and also leave the feeling it invoked. The feeling of connection and oneness with God does not have to leave, ever. In fact, it will benefit your children to create this sacred space wherever you go, most importantly within your home.

You may feel more of a spiritual connection in a designated sacred place outside of your normal lifestyle. However God is truly with you and has never left, as the illustration of the great sea shows. Therefore, God's presence does not only reside in places of worship, celebration or nature, but everywhere evenly and equally. The difference in the effect you feel from God's presence is dependent upon whether you acknowledge it and choose to participate with God who is already there.

➢ Please then, make your home a sanctuary as well as your temple or church.

➢ Make your place of business your sacred meeting place with God as well as your ashram or spiritual center.

Modify your environment so that it feels in alignment with your soul.

Own your power to be one with God in each place you go and in everything you do. Choose every day to be filled with miracles and invite God to be with you in each moment. Teach this to your children and be an example of consciously loving and celebrating God in all ways, all the time. Show children there is a reason to be inspired by life, all of life, because in all life is the presence of God. Help children understand, "Since God does not judge who to love and be present with neither do we. God is everywhere, even in things that hurt us and make us sad or angry."

Believe that your time with your children is a very special time to show them how they are connected, powerful souls. When they recognize this, they will be free from much of the challenge that this world brings to them. You are brave for giving them a passport to freedom.

It is hard as a parent in today's world to give your child fearless living when there is so much to be aware of. As essential as freedom is, with it comes responsibility. When educating about the *real world*, give children the knowledge and awareness to guide them. Fear not to share the imbalances of the world. Share truth, for truth is growth and power.

In the presence of God anything is possible, as seen with miracles. *Miracles* are when God uses its authority to directly affect your life; such a change may violate universal laws. This would only happen if God deems the change in your best interest for your spiritual growth. It is rare but miracles happen.

God participates on a subtle scale in your life through vast resources available to God, which include guides, other people, animals, songs, wind, sea, earth, fire, air, stars, moon, sun and other elements of creation. The point is that even if a classical miracle is not occurring, it does not mean that God is not helping you. God is always helping. To see the broader picture of how God is assisting you in every moment, please examine the relationship that a soul has with God and how you can feel this connection.

God is the Source of your life. Just as you have an umbilical cord with your mother prior to birth, you have an umbilical cord with your soul during your life, and your soul has an umbilical cord with God during its existence.

God is your eternal mother and father, and from a greater perspective God can be felt as such.

- When you receive food, shelter, water and sustenance, be grateful to God.

- When you wake up from sleep and you are breathing and living, thank God.

- When your child hugs you or a friend calls to see how you are, thank God.

God is the giver; your requirement is only to receive, and by giving to another you are sharing with God.

Chapter 23

COMMUNICATING WITH SPIRITUAL GUIDES

C hildren may already be seeing and talking with their nonphysical *spiritual guides* or other *spirits*. Please nurture this. Share with children that just as they have friends and family with bodies, they also have friends and family without bodies. Say to them, "These bodiless beings will give you guidance and play with you, among many other things. You can ask them for help and listen to their advice."

Because children's minds are more open than adults it is often easier for them to accept and communicate with their spirit guides and other spirits. Often children will have *imaginary* or *invisible* friends, and adults may look down on this or tell them these friends are not real. Instead of dismissing these experiences, ask kids to share them with you so you can be informed of their development as well as the names of their spirit guides.

When you talk with children about spirits please dispel the myths that are out there. Share with them, "There is only *good*. God has not created anything *bad*. It is people who create *bad* and *evil*. People create all the terrible things in the world that people experience, not God and not spirits, for all spirits created by God follow universal laws." Help your children understand that no spirit will manipulate or go against another soul's highest benefit. Therefore, there is no force created by God that will attempt to deceive or take you off path. If you experience such things, they are projections from your own thinking. If children learn these basic facts about spirits, they will not fear them. They will feel safe. They will own their power. Other people's energy will not be able to imbalance them. For when someone knows there is only good in God's creation, they will only experience good and will feel safe. There is no existence of demons, devils, negative spirits, poltergeists or any other manipulative phenomenon, except what is created by the thoughts of people. Thoughts can be tremendously powerful and manifest the experience of such things, as *thoughtforms*, but thought creations have no power over a person other than the power one gives to them.

This world is one of infinite possibilities including the possibility of creating something to fight or the experience of something harmful. As your children get acquainted with their guides and bodiless friends, encourage them to share their experiences with you so you can monitor them. As a result of the conditioning in the world, many kids accept thought-forms like aliens, monsters and the boogeyman. When a child believes in these things and fears them, the fear perpetuates the thought-forms and increases their strength and affect on the child. Changing their beliefs will eliminate their fears and the thought-forms will disappear.

A child can always ask God to come to assist them and God will help. When they learn who their guides are and ask them for help, the guides will help. All one needs to do is ask God to make the unwanted things leave and they will go away if the person *believes* they will. Also there is no real spirit that can stay and communicate with you if you demand it to go, under the law of free will. Therefore, you are in complete power over what you experience. There is no being or thought-form in existence that has domain over you without your permission—Not Even God.

This information is essential for really comprehending reality and letting go of misunderstood phenomenon that has been passed down for millennia. Feel comfortable knowing that nothing in creation decides your fate or controls your future but you. This allows you to be responsible for every experience you have and each choice you make. This reveals the *power* of your soul.

Chapter 24

STEPPING INTO THE SHOES OF CHILDREN

I n order to understand children you must first step into their shoes. To do this, truly desire it and use the tools in this book to see the world through their eyes. Children have a completely different experience with life than adults do. Not because they are children and you are an adult, but because adults require children to change at some point. I call this the *breaking point*.

The breaking point is when the child forfeits their way of perceiving things to accommodate the adult who is caring for them. This robs children of their natural innocence and is where children learn to love conditionally and accept conditionally, which devastates their development for the rest of their lives.

The breaking of a child is almost automatic in today's world.

I intend to bring awareness of how children view you and how you can accommodate their natural *love* and *innocence* so that the breaking point does not happen to them. If you honor the child's free will and follow the guidance in this book and books to follow, you should be able to save the child from breaking.

When a child breaks and changes because of how you want them to be and how you want them to perceive the world, they lose a part of themselves. When they change, they accept a belief about life telling them to accept your version of life instead of being free to create their own. Through finding the *root experience* of where they accepted the beliefs that broke them, they can at some point change their experience of life and thus be free to once again create their own beliefs about life. This usually happens much later in life, generally after the age of forty. Adults typically do not go on the journey of changing their core beliefs before they are forty years old.

If your child already accepted another person's version of life, you will know this by their behavior physically and emotionally. For a period of time the personality of the child will attempt to reclaim that freedom of expression. The severity of the belief that was forced onto the child by the caretaker will determine how they demonstrate their new version of life. With the tools in this book you may find the belief and change it, thereby freeing the child.

If you honor children and nurture who they are, they will develop into loving beings. It will save children years of clearing traumas caused by the adult's forced perspectives upon them. This will change the course of humanity's current path. The breaking point is the greatest trauma a child endures.

- Love children no matter what they do.

- Accept children no matter what they do.

- Encourage children to be comfortable with change; be an example of it.

- When children cry, encourage them to express themselves.

- When they laugh, cheer them on and laugh with them.

- When they are angry, listen to what they are really expressing behind their emotions; intuitively listen to their message.

- When children disagree, allow them to disagree and attempt to understand their perspective.

You will be surprised how wise children are because of the innate simplicity that functions within them.

- Learn with kids how to embrace your emotions and thoughts.

- Make games out of everything. Make disagreeing and sharing fun. Everything can be fun and safe. Create safety in their environment.

- Bring people into their lives who embrace these ideas.

- Enroll children in schools that embrace a new way of teaching.

- Teach your family and friends how to be with your child in a soul-based way.

- When people bring imbalances into an environment, share with the child why they behave in imbalanced ways and that everyone is doing the best they can.

- Be consistent so the energy is congruent between what you say and what you actually do.

- If you mean something, express it clearly so children will learn how to express themselves clearly.

- If children have a challenging time with others at school, educate them that kids learn what they do from their parents, other adults and other kids.

- Help children be responsible for the friends they bring into their life.

- If a child has a conflict at school or elsewhere, and it seems insignificant, please do not judge it as small. Whether it seems small or large, important or unimportant to you, if a child shares it with you it is important and big to them. Listen to them. Most things are big to children, even if they don't express the importance of them. Listen to children.

- Listen To Children. Really Listen.

- Do the best you can to become as a child and step into their shoes. Imagine yourself in this amazing yet conflicting world as a child.

- When you act or respond, first put yourself in the child's shoes to feel and sense how they will see and feel you responding to them.

- Take the time to really care and stop your life for just one moment to pay attention. The busyness of the average adult life makes it difficult to really pay attention to kids. Make time, change your life, rearrange your schedule and reset your first priority.

➤ Are the children in your life truly your priority?

- Get real with your situation as a teacher, parent, caretaker, babysitter, doctor, friend, family member or bystander of children. Require yourself to re-think, re-feel, re-see and remember your innocence and connection with kids.

The youth are the most important component and invest-ment that this world has to create a new world. They are your ticket to freedom as a civilization on Earth. They are the very blood of life itself.

Pray you will change and ask God to help you . . . it is hap-pening . . . you have been answered . . .

Decide today is your day. Decide now is your time.

Ask God to give you guidance and expect a different life for you and your loved ones . . . expect a different life for the children of today.

Made in the USA
Lexington, KY
16 October 2012